STRUCTURAL
DETAILS
FOR WOOD
CONSTRUCTION

Companion Volumes

Newman • Structural Details for Concrete Construction
Newman • Structural Details for Masonry Construction
Newman • Structural Details for Steel Construction

STRUCTURAL DETAILS FOR WOOD CONSTRUCTION

Morton Newman, P.E.

PROJECT EDITOR: Jeremy Robinson

McGRAW-HILL BOOK COMPANY

New York St. Louis San Francisco Auckland
Bogotá Hamburg London Madrid Mexico
Milan Montreal New Delhi Panama
Paris São Paulo Singapore
Sydney Tokyo Toronto

Library of Congress Cataloging-in-Publication Data

Newman, Morton.
  Structural details for wood construction.

  "The material in this volume has been published
previously in Standard structural details for building
construction"—T.p. verso.
  Includes index.
  1. Building, Wooden. 2. Building—Details—
Drawing. I. Newman, Morton. Standard structural
details for building contruction. II. Title.
TH1101.N425 1988   694   87-21369
ISBN 0-07-046358-1 (pbk.)

1234567890   KGP/KGP 8903210987

ISBN 0-07-046358-1

Printed and bound by Arcata Graphics/Kingsport

To my mother

Contents

About This Book   *ix*

Preface   *xi*

Abbreviations   *xiii*

INTRODUCTION   1

DETAILS   7
Post base connections   **Floor sheathing**   **Wood stairs**
Walls   **Floor framing**   **Post and beam connections**
Beam connections   **Glued, laminated wood details**

Index   *121*

About This Book

Since publication in 1968, over 30,000 copies of the hardcover edition of Morton Newman's STANDARD STRUCTURAL DETAILS FOR BUILDING CONSTRUCTION have been sold to architects, engineers, drafters, and others concerned with the design of building structure and the communication of that design to those responsible for accomplishing it in construction.

Now the publishers have made it possible for persons interested in one particular type of structure—wood, concrete, masonry, or steel—to purchase just the section or sections of *Standard Structural Details* which they need. The hardcover book has been split up into four separate low-cost softcover editions:

Structural Details for Wood Construction
Structural Details for Concrete Construction
Structural Details for Masonry Construction
Structural Details for Steel Construction

In this book, the designer will find a host of proven designs in time-tested details for post base connections; floor sheathing; wood stairs; walls; floor framing; post and beam connections; beam connections; and glued, laminated wood details.

Introductory material has been revised to reflect code changes since the original edition, and each page of details appears on the right, while facing pages incorporate a preprinted grid for drawings, notes, and ideas the reader may wish to preserve.

Preface

The purpose of this series of books is to provide a graphic means of communication between architects, engineers, contractors, and students who are engaged in the design and construction of buildings. The four basic structural materials that are employed in building construction are wood, concrete, masonry, and steel. In the application of these materials many standard details and methods of construction have been developed. For several years the author found it quite useful to collect and index standard structural details for the preparation of structural drawings of buildings. The use of structural graphic standards reduced the cost of production of structural drawings and also helped to facilitate the communication of information between all of the personnel who were involved in the design and construction of a building. No claim is made for the originality of the details in these books as they are standard methods of construction and they are extensively used throughout the construction industry.

These books consist of a series of drawings of standard structural details that are most frequently employed in building construction. The details are presented individually and in their most basic and general form. A brief description is given for each detail pertaining to the material used, the type of condition shown, and its method of construction. In no instance should a book be considered or used as a substitute for the engineer or as a shortcut method of engineering. It is the function of the engineer to verify the use of any detail and to determine the sizes, dimensions, and all other pertinent information that will be essential to its use in a particular building design. The details are separated and arranged into four books with respect to the type of construction materials used: wood, concrete, masonry, or steel. In some instances two types of construction materials are used in the same detail. The author endeavored to place each detail in the related book and in the sequence of its use in building construction so that it could be readily located. Also, the index for this book has been set up so that any particular detail that may be sought can be easily located.

The engineering information presented in these books is in accordance with the basic requirements of The American Institute of Steel Construction, The American Concrete Institute, The International Conference of Building Officials Uniform Building Code, "The West Coast Lumbermen's Douglas Fir Use Book," and The Concrete Masonry Association of California. Standard details and construction methods evolve from the structural design requirements. Many excellent books on structural design and analysis are available to the practicing engineer and student; there is also a great need for applied practical information related to structural drafting and the use of construction materials. Expanding technology in the fields of building engineering and construction has created a situation which demands that the structural drawings be more complete and therefore more complex.

The purpose of structural drawings is to communicate the engineer's design requirements to the various contractors and material fabricators.

To achieve total communication, the structural drawings should be clear and complete, the general presentation of information should be in a logical sequence, all sections and details should be shown and clearly referenced, and any field conditions should be considered on the drawings. A good set of structural drawings will ensure that the building is constructed in accordance with the engineering design requirements and that construction delays and unnecessary additional costs are avoided.

The engineer's work is the prime factor in the successful design and construction of a building; however, in the final event, his or her work is directly dependent upon the intelligence and integrity of the workers on the construction job, particularly at the supervisory level. Poor fieldwork in terms of accuracy and material quality control will negate a great deal of engineering effort. Building construction requires a high degree of teamwork between the engineers and the contractors. Each party should have a working knowledge of the other's functions and responsibilities. The author hopes that these books will serve as communication tools that will improve the quality of engineering and construction. Also, engineering and architectural students can use this book as a source of information to familiarize themselves with the methods and materials of construction. As students use the information presented in these books they will increase their ability to translate structural engineering calculations into practical applications.

I would like to acknowledge the very able assistance of Bruce L. Ward, who drew the details shown on the following pages and assisted in assembling the information into book form. Also, I would like to thank Jack Clark for his advice and encouragement and acknowledge the assistance of Bogdan Todorovic in the early stages of these books.

Morton Newman
Civil Engineer

Abbreviations

Adjustable	Adjust.	Existing	Exist.
Alternate	Alt.	Expand	Exp.
American Concrete Institute	A.C.I.	Expose	Expo.
American Institute of Steel Construction	A.I.S.C.	Exterior	Ext.
American Society of Testing and Materials	A.S.T.M.	Fillet	Fill.
		Finish	Fin.
Architect	Arch.	Floor	Flr.
Area	A.	Foot	Ft.
		Footing	Ftg.
Beam	Bm.	Foundation	Fdn.
Block	Blk.	Framing	Frmg.
Blocking	Blkg.		
Bottom	Bott.	Gauge	Ga.
Building	Bldg.	Glued Laminated	Gl. Lam.
		Grade	Gr.
Calculations	Calcs.	Grout	Grt.
Ceiling	Ceil.	Gypsum	Gyp.
Cement	Cem.		
Center Line	C.L.	Hanger	Hngr.
Channel Stud	C.S.	Height	Ht.
Civil Engineer	C.E.	Hook	Hk.
Clear	Clr.	Horizontal	Horiz.
Column	Col.		
Concrete	Conc.		
Connection	Conn.	Inch	In.
Construction	Constr.	Inclusive	Incl.
Continuous	Cont.	Inside Diameter	I.D.
Cubic	Cu.	Interior	Int.
Deflection	Defl.	Joint	Jnt.
Depression	Depr.	Joist	Jst.
Detail	Det.		
Diagonal	Diag.	Lag Screw	L.S.
Diameter	Dia.	Laminated	Lam.
Dimension	Dim.	Lateral	Lat.
Discontinuous	Disc.	Light Weight	Lt. Wt.
Double	Dbl.		
Drawing	Drwg.	Machine	Mach.
		Masonry	Mas.
Each	Ea.	Maximum	Max.
Elevation	El. or Elev.	Membrane	Memb.
Engineer	Engr.	Metal	Met. or Mtl.
Equal	Eq.	Minimum	Min.
Equipment	Equip.	Moment of Inertia	I

Nails	d (penny)	Sheathing	Shtg.
Natural	Nat.	Sheet	Sht.
Number	No. or #	Spacing	Spcg.
		Specification	Spec.
On Center	O.C.	Spiral	Sp.
Opening	Opng.	Stagger	Stgr.
Opposite	Opp.	Standard	Std.
Outside Diameter	O.D.	Steel	Stl.
		Steel Joist	S.J.
Panels	Pnls.	Stiffener	Stiff.
Partition	Part.	Stirrup	Stirr.
Penetration	Pen.	Structural	Struct.
Plaster	Plas.	Structural Steel Tube	S.S.T.
Plate	Pl.	Square	Sq.
Plywood	Plywd.	Symmetrical	Sym.
Pounds per Cubic Foot	P.C.F.		
Pounds per Square Foot	P.S.F.	Thick	Thk.
Pounds per Square Inch	P.S.I.	Through	Thru.
Pressure	Press.	Tread	Tr.
Radius	R.	Ultimate	Ult.
Rafter	Rftr.	Ultimate Stress Design	U.S.D.
Rectangular	Rect.	Uniform Building Code	U.B.C.
Reinforcing	Reinf.	Utility	Util.
Required	Reqd.		
Riser	R.	Vertical	Vert.
Roof	Rf.	Volume	Vol.
Room	Rm.		
Round	ϕ	Waterproof	W.P.
		Weight	Wt.
Schedule	Sched.	Welded Wire Fabric	W.W.F.
Section	Sect.	Wide Flange	W.F.
Section Modulus	S.	With	W/
Seismic	Seis.	Working Stress Design	W.S.D.

INTRODUCTION

The details presented in this volume pertain generally to buildings of wood frame construction. The drawings are arranged in the sequence of their use in the construction of a building. The general categories of the details are post and footing connections, floor and roof structural diaphragms, stair sections and details, wood stud wall sections and connections, roof framing sections, beam and floor connections and sections, post and beam connections, lateral force connections of beams to wood stud walls, wood framing and steel beam connections, and glued laminated wood or heavy timber details.

The species of wood used in the drawings is not designated, since the availability of the different species of wood used in construction varies for each particular geographic region. Local building codes or the applicable construction design criteria specify the allowable working stress values for each species of wood used. Building codes also regulate the control of structural lumber by requiring stress grade marks from a responsible agency on each member and on plywood panels. The allowable stress requirement of wood members is only one of the factors that is involved in the use of wood as a structural material. Protection against moisture and decay may be necessary,

depending on the climate conditions in which the wood is used. Wood will not be subject to decay when the moisture content is less than 20%; however, decay caused by excessive moisture will definitely occur when the moisture content is greater than 25%. The following structural details of foundations are drawn to eliminate the possibility of excessive moisture in the floor joists. Wood mudsills or ledgers that are in contact with concrete or masonry should be pressure-treated or constructed of a species of naturally durable lumber. Also, interior floors, ceilings, and attic spaces should be ventilated to eliminate moisture condensation. Another source of damage to wood structures is the presence of termites. The termite is an insect similar to the ant that can destroy wood by devouring the cellulose material. Attacks by large numbers of termites can be prevented by creating a barrier between the ground moisture and the wood members. Termite barriers are made of 26-gauge galvanized sheet metal and are installed to protect the top of the foundation from the ground surface. There are also many commercial chemical solutions that can be added to the adjacent ground to prevent termite intrusion. Since lumber is susceptible to decay from moisture and termites, it must also be protected while it is stored on the job site prior to its use in the construction. This can be accomplished by maintaining the lumber at least 6″ above the ground surface and keeping it covered with a waterproof material.

Wood structural framing requires that the members be accurately cut to size and fit together with even bearing surfaces. Special care should be taken in the design and the construction to allow for wood shrinkage and the deflections of the members. The wood members used in the details in this chapter are mill-cut to standard sizes; however, they are designated by their nominal, or rough, size. Table 1 gives the nominal dimension and the net dimension of wood members with four sides surfaced.

The details in this chapter are used for commercial and residential wood-framed structures. The roof and the floors are framed with rafters or joists, which are usually spaced 12″, 16″, or 24″ apart, depending on their span, the unit load on the member, and the allowable working stress of the wood. When the rafters or joists are used to support plaster ceilings, the deflection of the members should be limited to prevent surface cracks. The floor and roof framing members should have an end bearing length of 1½″ on wood or metal and 3″ on concrete or masonry, except as shown in Detail 14. The floor joists should be laterally braced by blocking or cross bridging as shown in Detail 8. The distance between rows of bridging should not exceed 8′0″. The end blocking or rim joists, as shown in Details 15, 16, and 21 through 24, may be used to brace the floor joists laterally at the walls. Floor joists

may be notched for piping, provided the notch does not exceed ⅙ of the depth of the joist and is not located within the middle ⅓ of the span. Holes may be bored in floor joists for piping or electrical cable, provided the hole is not closer than 2″ from the top or the bottom of the joist. When floor joists are notched at the ends, the notch should not exceed ¼ of the joist depth. Wood subfloors are nailed to the top of the floor joists as shown in Details 7 and 10. Detail 9(a) shows a special type of roof sheathing for prefabricated panelized roof construction.

Interior and exterior walls of wood buildings are constructed with vertical studs. The size and spacing of the studs (bearing or non-bearing wall) depend on the load to be supported by the wall, the height of the wall, and the lateral forces normal to the surface of the wall. Interior partitions or non-bearing walls may be constructed with 2″ × 4″ studs spaced at 24″ o.c.; however, studs are usually spaced at 16″ o.c. to accommodate the wall-covering materials. Non-bearing partitions are supported by double floor joists as shown in Detail 10 and are connected at the top to the floor joists or rafters as shown in Detail 19(a) and (b). Exterior walls and bearing walls are framed with 2″ × 4″ studs at 24″ o.c. for one-story buildings, 2″ × 4″ studs at 16″ o.c. for two-story buildings. When the stud height is greater than 6′0″ and it is supporting loads from two stories above, the studs should be 2″ × 6″ or 3″ × 4″ at 16″ o.c. The studs in exterior walls and bearing walls should be placed with the larger dimension perpendicular to the wall. The bottoms of the studs are nailed to a sole plate 2″ thick and equal to the depth of the studs; the tops of the studs are connected to a double 2″ plate as shown in Detail 26. Stud walls should be continuously blocked at mid-height as a fire stop. Stud wall corners and intersections should be framed with at least three studs nailed together to make a solid member. The walls are laterally braced by 1″ × 4″ let-in braces spaced not more than 25′0″ o.c. and set at each corner and intersection of the walls.

Details 7 and 9(a) and (b) are specifically concerned with plywood as a roof or floor sheathing material. Douglas fir

Table 1. Standard Lumber Dimensions—S4S

Nominal or rough dimension, in.	Surfaced, dry	Surfaced, unseasoned
1	¾	¹³⁄₁₆
2	1½	1⁹⁄₁₆
3	2½	2⁹⁄₁₆
4	3½	3⁹⁄₁₆
6	5½	5⅝
8	7¼	7½
10	9¼	9½
12	11¼	11½
Over 12	Off ¾	Off ½

Based on WWPA 1970 Rules.

plywood panels are manufactured by laminating and gluing together an odd number of layers of Douglas fir veneer sheets. The veneer sheets are usually ⅛" thick and are laminated so that the surface grain of the adjacent layers are perpendicular to each other. Standard plywood panels are 48" × 96" with the exposed surface grain on each side running in the direction of the length of the panel. The strength of the wood running in the direction of the surface grain of the panel is much greater than the strength of the cross-grain plies, which only serve as a filler material between the laminations; therefore, plywood should be placed so that the surface grain is perpendicular to the framing members. Two types of Douglas fir plywood are manufactured, interior-type and exterior-type plywood, their classification depending on the glue used in their fabrication. The exterior-type plywood uses a waterproof adhesive. Structural plywood is designated as Structural I or II C-D INT APA for interiors, and Structural I or II C-C EXT APA for exterior use. Vertical and horizontal structural diaphragms are constructed by nailing the plywood panels to the framing members. The capacity of the diaphragm to resist lateral force depends on the thickness of the plywood, the size and spacing of the nails to the panel edges and the diaphragm edges, and the panel-edge blocking.

Details 86(a) to 95 are drawings of glued laminated wood or heavy timber construction. Building codes specify heavy timber as structural wood members of sufficient width and depth to qualify as slow-burning construction. The fire rating for heavy timber varies in different building codes; however, the National Board of Fire Underwriters recommends the following nominal dimensions for heavy-timber construction: columns shall not be less than 8" in any dimension; beams and girders shall not be less than 6" in width or 10" in depth; floors shall be constructed of tongue and grooved planks not less than 3" thick and covered with 1" thick flooring laid perpendicular or diagonal to the subfloor planks; roof sheathing shall be not less than 3" thick tongue and grooved planks.

Glued laminated wood members are often used for heavy timber construction since their nominal dimensions can readily conform to building-code requirements. These members are factory fabricated and consist of vertically laminated, nominal 2" thick boards of various combinations of structural lumber, each board being glued to the adjacent board. Two types of adhesives are used in the manufacture of glued laminated structural members. When the moisture content of the member exceeds 15% or when it is exposed to the weather, the boards are laminated with an exterior-type phenol-resorcinol glue. A fortified casein glue is used to fabricate members that are used in the interior of a building or that are not exposed to excessive moisture. The allowable working stresses of glued laminated structural members depend on the number of laminations and the structural grade of the laminated boards. Since these members are manufactured to meet the engineer's design requirements, it is recommended that they be shop-drawn and detailed before they are fabricated.

Quite often glued laminated wood members are left exposed to attain an architecutral effect. In such instances the finished appearance of the wood is important and should be specified as either architectural or premium-finished. Also, the member should be delivered to the job site in a protective wrapping which should not be removed until after the member is in place. Glued laminated members that are not used in an exposed situation may have an industrial-finished appearance and need only a protective wrapping against excessive moisture.

Wood framing members and floor sheathing that are nominally 1" and 2" in width are connected by wire nails. Common wire nails are most often used in framed construction, although other types of nails are available where stronger withdrawal-type connections may be required. Nails are generally employed to react principally in shear caused by lateral loading of the connection. The lateral resistance value of a nail depends on the nail diameter and the depth of penetration into the member to be joined. When a force is applied parallel to the nail, a withdrawal resistance will occur which is much less than the lateral resistance; therefore, this type of connection should be avoided. Nails that are driven into a member at an angle of approximately 30° to the surface grain are called toenails and will have $\frac{2}{3}$ of the normal lateral-resistance value. Nails should penetrate the connected member at least $\frac{1}{2}$ the length of the nail, all connections should have at least two nails, and nails should be at least $\frac{1}{2}$ the nail length apart and be not less than $\frac{1}{4}$ of the nail length from the edge of the member. Many of the drawings in this volume call for metal clips. These clips are a commercially standard piece of hardware and are commonly used to join wood members when a high connection resistance is required. The clips are made of 18-gauge sheet metal in various left- and right-hand configurations and are basically used for light wood framed connections. Table 2 shows the various common wire nail sizes and lengths. Table 3 gives the recommended light-framed nailing schedule for the different types of connections. Plywood roof and floor sheathing nails are not specified in this table since they are determined by the shear to be resisted by the diaphragm.

The use of metal bolts to connect wood members to each other and to other structural materials such as concrete, masonry, and steel is a common and economical method of construction. Bolts connecting wood members are capable of resisting forces applied both parallel and lateral to the shank of the bolt by bearing and shear. In the following drawings in this chapter the bolts are used to connect metal plates to wood posts and beams, to connect wood members to each other, and to connect wood framing to steel beams. Flat wash-

Table 3. Recommended Nailing Schedule

Connection	Nailing	Nail size, d
Joist to sill or girder	Toenail	2–16
Bridging to joist	Toenail	2–8
1 × 6 subfloor to joist	Face nail	2–8
2 subfloor to joist or girder	—	2–16
Plate to joist or blocking	—	16 at 16″ O.C.
Stud to plate	End nail	2–16
Stud to plate	Toenail	3–16 or 4–8
Top plates spike together:		
Laps and intersections	—	16 at 24″ O.C.
Ceiling joists:		
To plate	Toenail	2–16
Laps over partitions	Toenail	3–16
To parallel alternate rafters	Toenail	3–16
Rafter to plate	—	3–16
Continuous 1″ brace to stud	—	2–8
2″ cut in bracing to stud	—	2–16
1″ sheathing to bearing	—	2–8
Corner studs and angles	—	16 at 30″ O.C.

ers should be used in bolted wood connections when metal side plates are not specifically designated.

The washers are either round or square and are made of malleable iron. The size and the thickness of a washer are determined by calculation and depend on the bolt tension when the bolt is tightened or loaded and on the bearing stress normal to the wood surface. Heavy timber construction often requires that the washers be made of cast iron; however, the washers are not designated in the following wood details. The strength of a bolted wood connection depends on the thickness of the members, the number and the size of the bolts, the species of the wood, the angle of the resisted force to the grain of the members, the use of metal side plates or other standard hardware connectors, and the arrangement of the bolt spacing in the connection. It is important that the bolt spacing and the edge distance be sufficient to ensure that the wood will not split and to allow enough bearing area. Each bolt should be installed through a predrilled hole $\frac{1}{16}''$ larger than the bolt shank diameter.

Lag screws are often used in lieu of bolts when it is not possible or convenient to obtain full penetration by a bolt through a wood member. The capacity of lag screws to resist lateral forces and withdrawal depends on the

Table 2. Common Wire-Nail Sizes

Size of nail, d	Standard length, in.	Wire gauge
6	2	$11\frac{1}{2}$
8	$2\frac{1}{2}$	$10\frac{1}{4}$
10	3	9
12	$3\frac{1}{4}$	9
16	$3\frac{1}{2}$	8
20	4	6
30	$4\frac{1}{2}$	5
40	5	4
50	$5\frac{1}{2}$	3
60	6	2

same factors as do bolts in wood members; however, lag screws will not resist as much force as an equal size bolt. A lag screw should be installed in a predrilled hole approximately 70% of the shank diameter of the screw, and it should penetrate the member to be joined at least $\frac{1}{2}$ of the screw length or eight shank diameters.

In general, wood is a highly versatile and inexpensive construction material. Except for glued laminated members, wood can be fabricated and assembled on the job site. The contractor must have clear and complete structural drawings of the framing and connections to avoid the inefficient use of labor and materials.

DETAILS

Notes ▪ Drawings ▪ Ideas

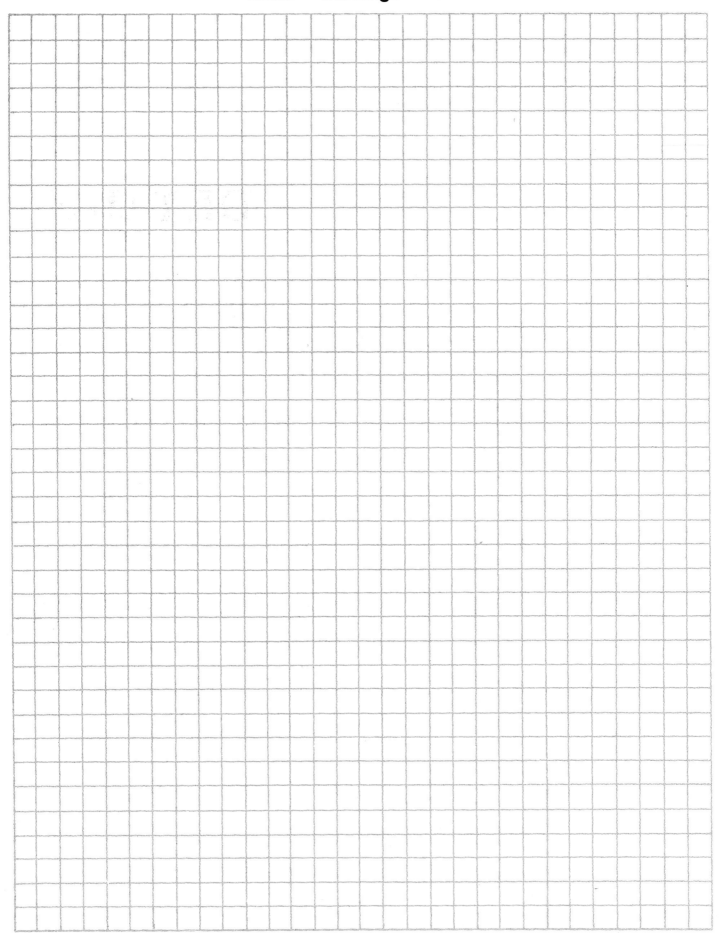

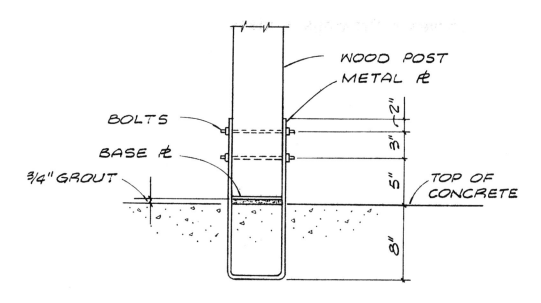

Detail 1(a). A wood post connected to a concrete foundation using a U-shaped metal plate bolted to the post and embedded in the concrete. The base plate should be the same size as the post.

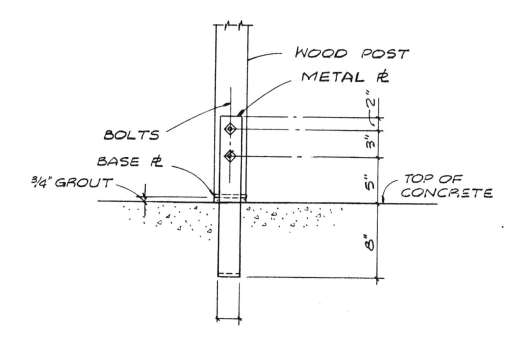

Detail 1(b). A side view of Detail 1(a). The length of the metal plate and the thickness of the bolts are determined by calculation.

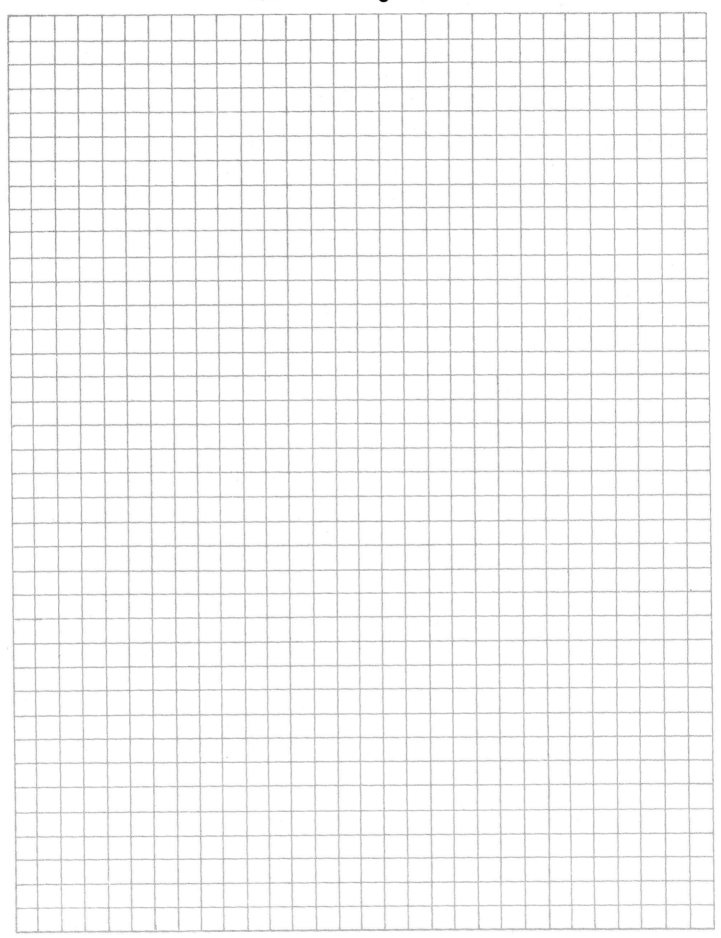

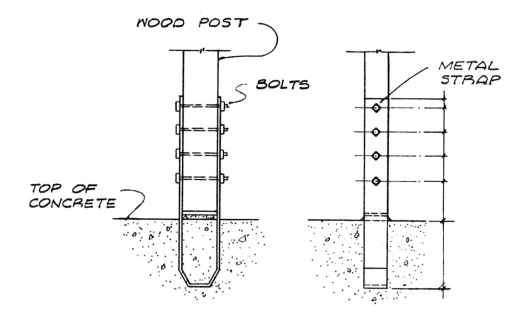

Detail 2. A wood-post connection to a concrete foundation using a U-shaped metal plate and bolts. The number of bolts and the size of the plate permit the post to resist tension or compression.

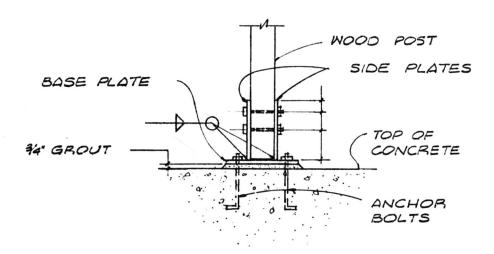

Detail 3. A wood-post connection to a concrete foundation. The metal side plates are bolted through the post and welded to the base plate.

Notes ▪ Drawings ▪ Ideas

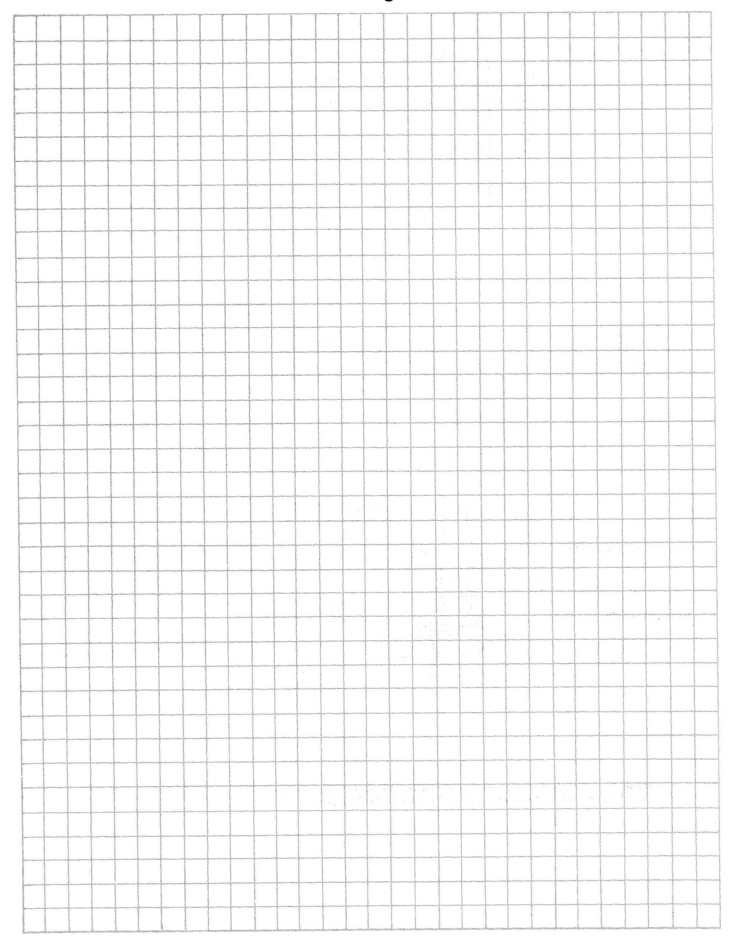

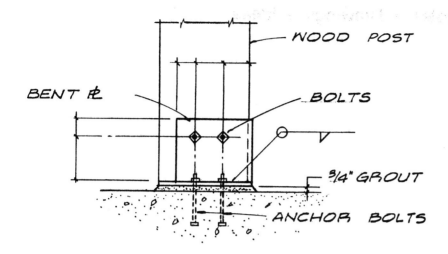

Detail 4(a). A wood-post connection to a concrete foundation. The metal shoe plate connection can resist lateral loads at the base of the post.

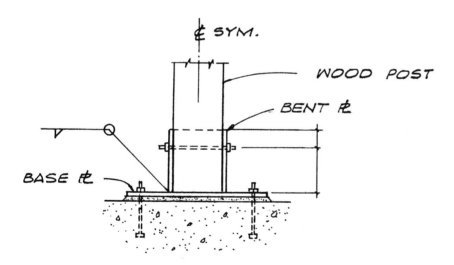

Detail 4(b). A front view of Detail 4(a).

Notes · Drawings · Ideas

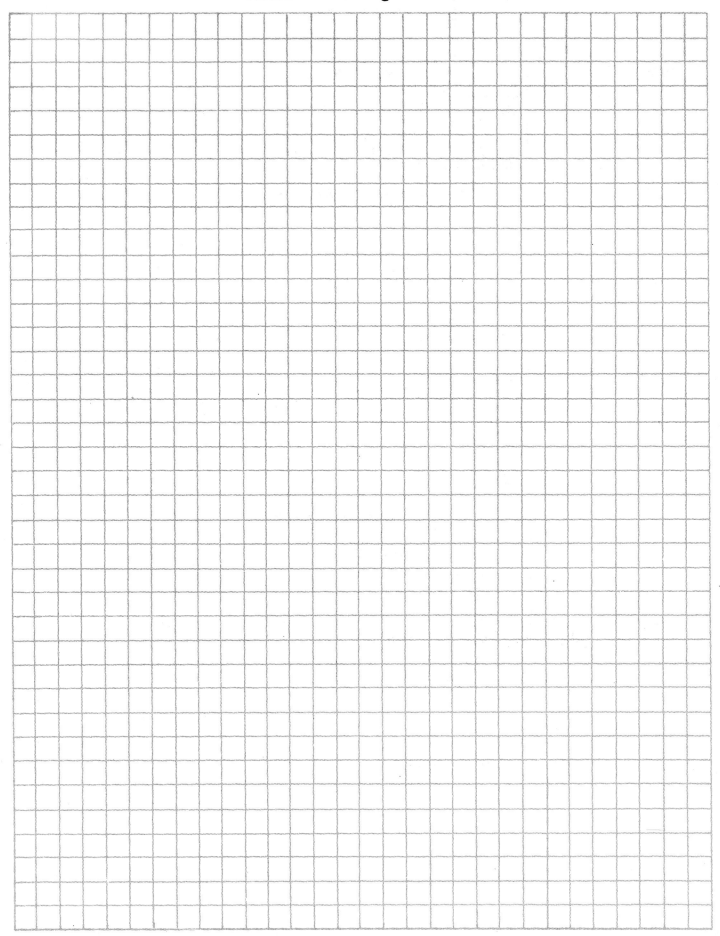

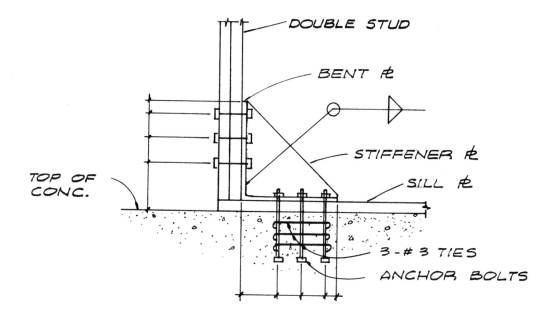

DOUBLE STUD

BENT ℞

STIFFENER ℞

SILL ℞

TOP OF CONC.

3 - # 3 TIES

ANCHOR BOLTS

Detail 5. A structural tie-down connection for ends or corners of wood stud walls that are used to resist lateral forces. The bolts through the double studs and into the concrete permit the wall to resist uplift forces caused by lateral loads applied parallel to the wall. The number of bolts and the size of metal plates are determined by calculation.

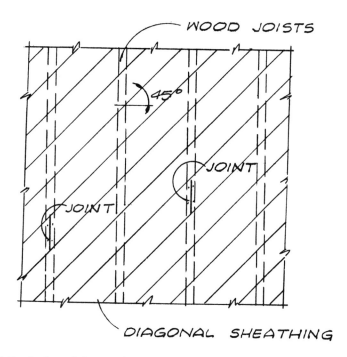

WOOD JOISTS

45°

JOINT

JOINT

DIAGONAL SHEATHING

Detail 6. A plan of diagnonal sheathing boards nailed to wood rafters or floor joists. The sheathing can act as a diaphragm to resist lateral force when it is nailed to the rafters or joists. The sheathing board should be 1″ × 6″ or 1″ × 8″ members, and the joints of adjacent boards should be separated by two rafters or joists. Each board should be nailed to a rafter or joist with a minimum of two 8d nails.

Notes ▪ Drawings ▪ Ideas

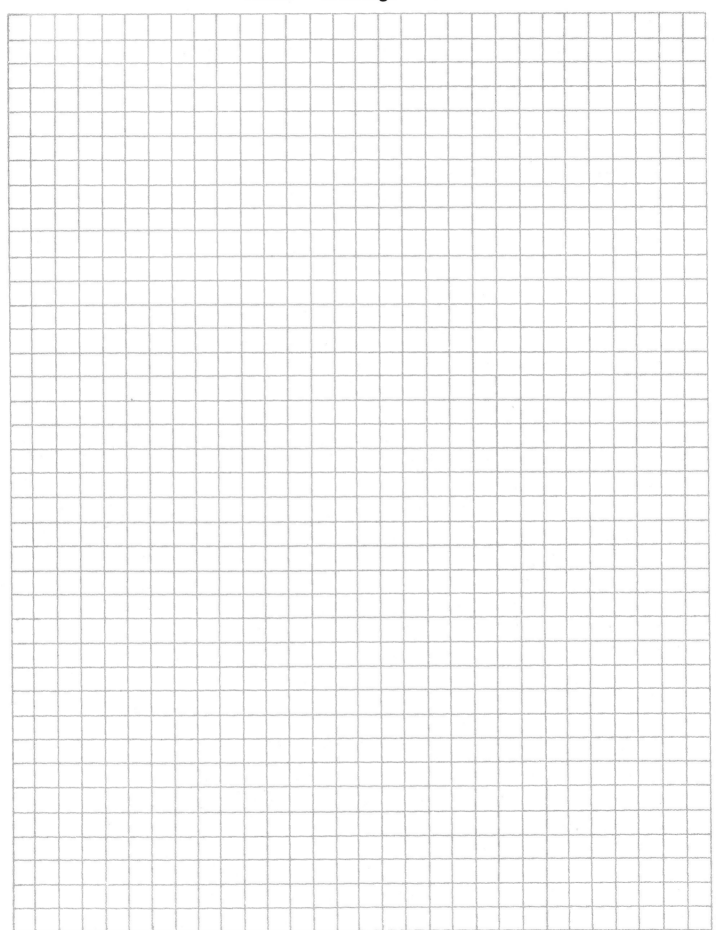

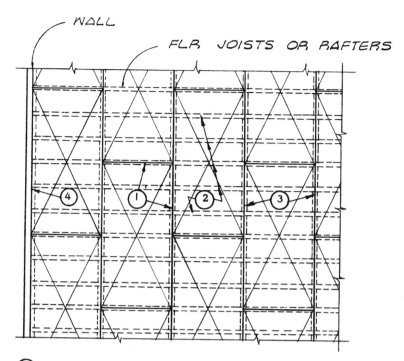

WALL

FLR JOISTS OR RAFTERS

① EDGE NAILING

② FIELD NAILING

③ PANEL EDGE TO BLOCKING

④ BOUNDARY NAILING

Detail 7. A plan of floor or roof sheathing using 4'0" × 8'0" plywood panels. The ability of the sheathing to act as a diaphragm to resist lateral force depends on the thickness of the plywood and the size and spacing of the nails. The numbers circled on the plan permit the nailing to be scheduled. The plywood is laid with the surface grain perpendicular to the framing members.

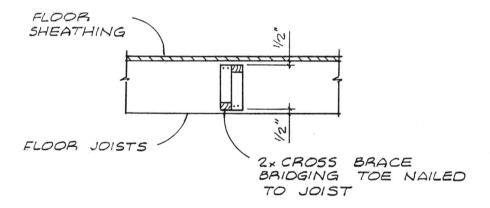

FLOOR SHEATHING

½"

FLOOR JOISTS

½"

2× CROSS BRACE BRIDGING TOE NAILED TO JOIST

Detail 8. A section of cross bracing acting as bridging between floor joists or roof rafters. The spacing of the rows of bridging is specified by the local building code.

Notes · Drawings · Ideas

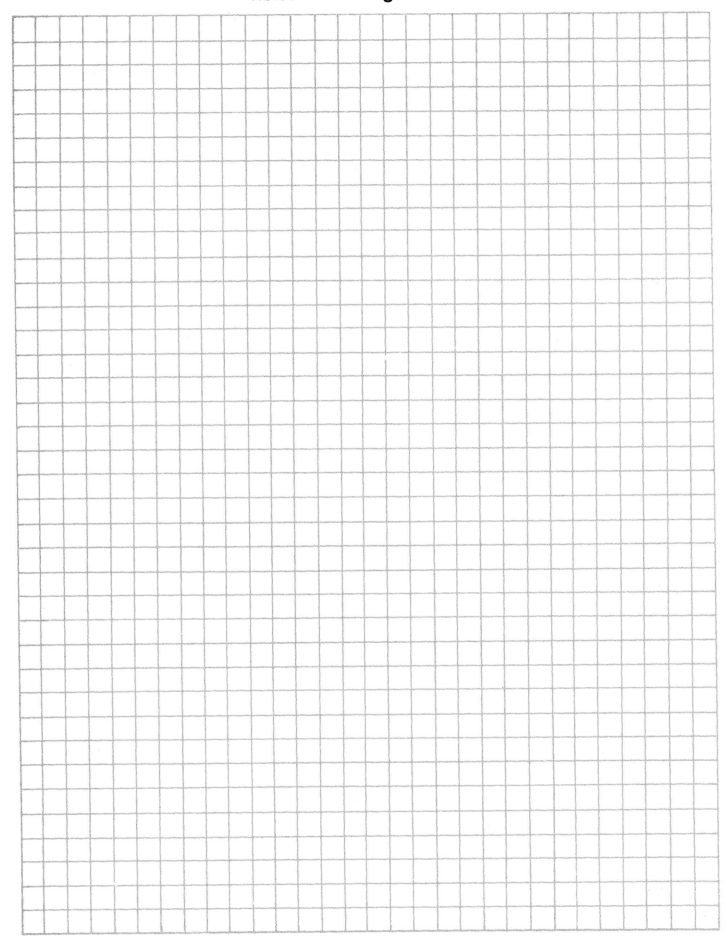

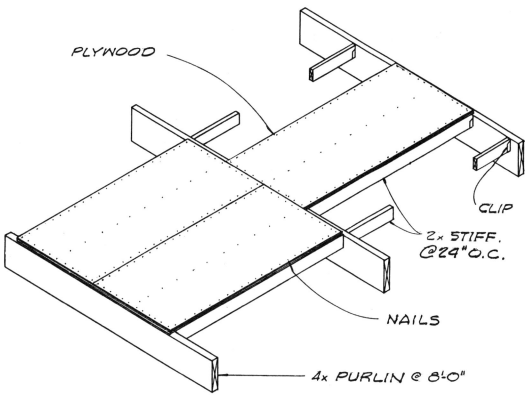

PLYWOOD

CLIP

2x STIFF.
@24"O.C.

NAILS

4x PURLIN @ 8'-0"

Details 9(a). An isometric view of a plywood panelized roof system. 4'0" × 8'0" plywood panels are delivered to the job site with prenailed 2" × 4" wood stiffeners nailed to the edge and to the middle of the panel. The panels are installed and nailed in place to the 4" wide wood purlins which are spaced at 8'0" o.c. The size and spacing of the nails to the purlin members depends on the required lateral resistance of the plywood sheathing acting as a diaphragm.

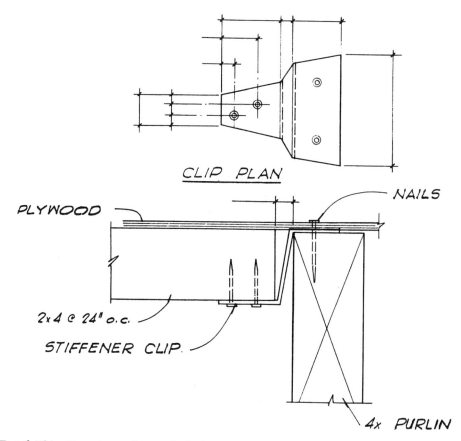

CLIP PLAN

NAILS

PLYWOOD

2x4 @ 24" o.c.

STIFFENER CLIP

4x PURLIN

Detail 9(b). Two views of a standard sheet metal clip used to connect the 2" × 4" stiffeners to the purlins shown in Detail 9(a). The size of the clip depends on the load to be supported on the roof.

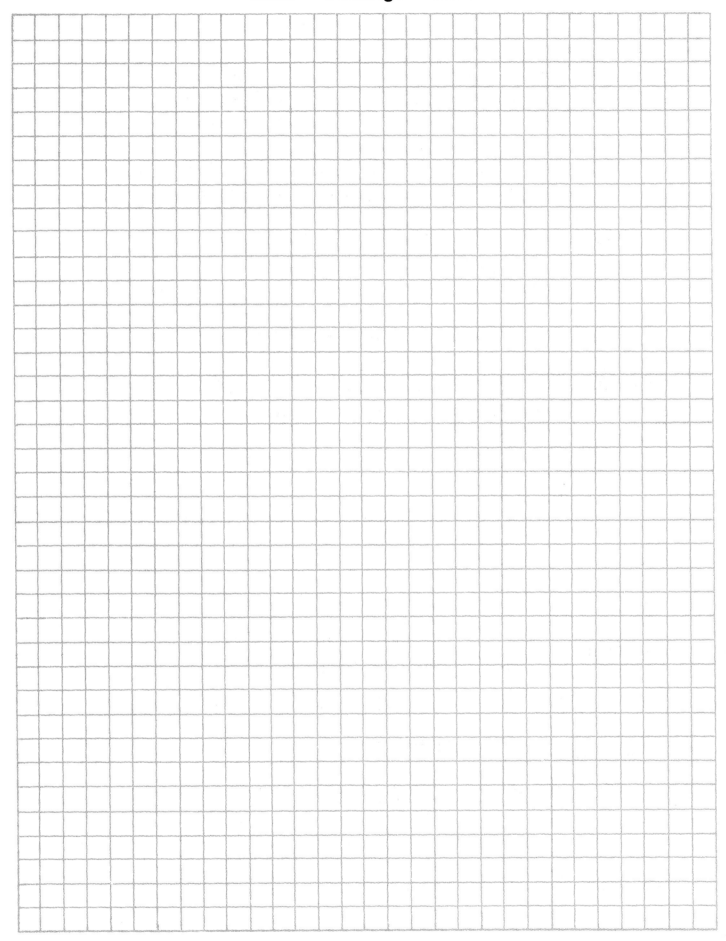

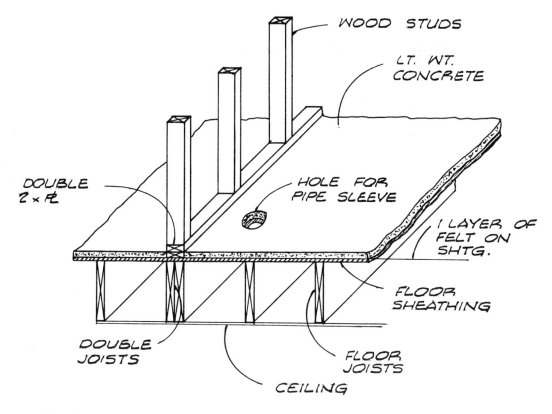

Detail 10. An isometric view of a wood floor with 1⅝″ thick concrete cover. Double joists are placed under the wood stud wall. The double plate at the base of the wood stud wall is optional; a single plate may be used. The plate at the base of the wood stud wall is used as a concrete screed. The concrete is poured over one layer of 15 lb. building felt.

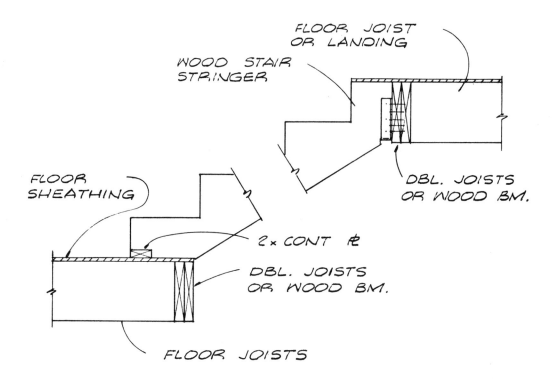

Detail 11. A section of a wood floor and stair stringer. The size and spacing of the wood stringers are determined by the load and span of the stairs. The base of the stringer is connected to the floor by toenailing the floor joist through the floor sheathing. The top of the stringer is connected to the double joist with a standard joist hanger.

Notes • Drawings • Ideas

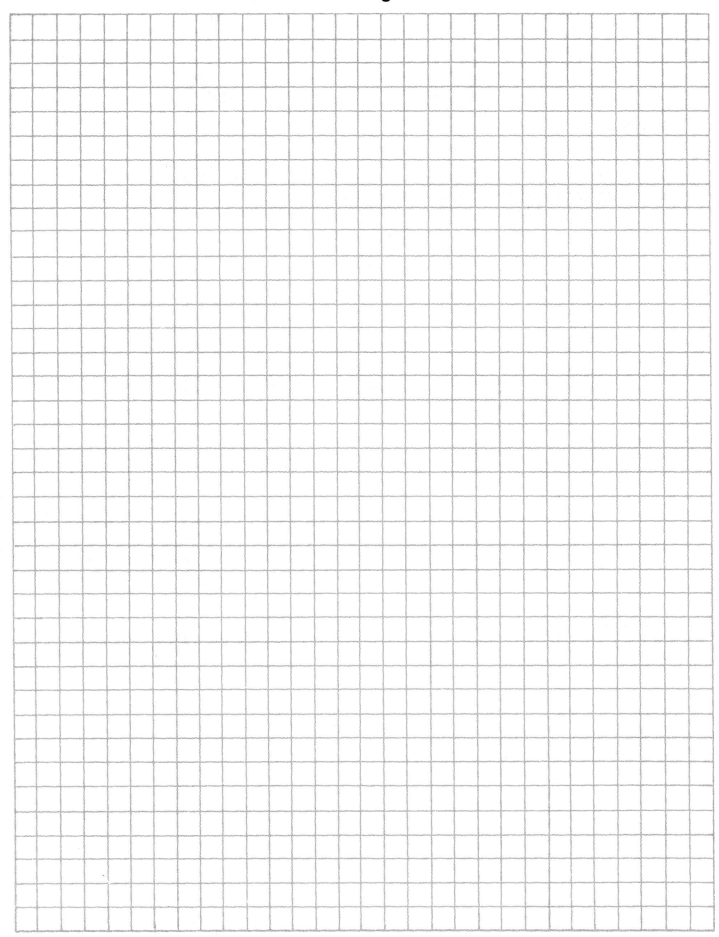

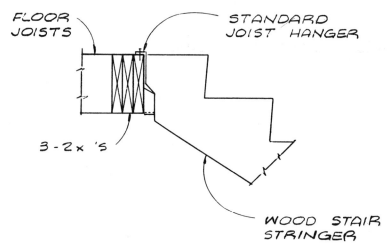

Detail 12. A section of a connection of a wood stringer to a triple-joist floor beam. The stringer is connected to the beam with a standard joist hanger.

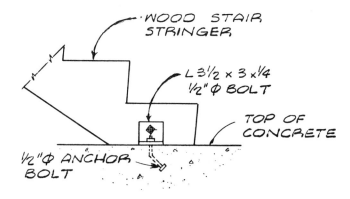

Detail 13. A connection of the base of a wood stringer to a concrete floor slab. Each stringer is connected to the concrete slab by a clip angle with one bolt through each leg of the angle.

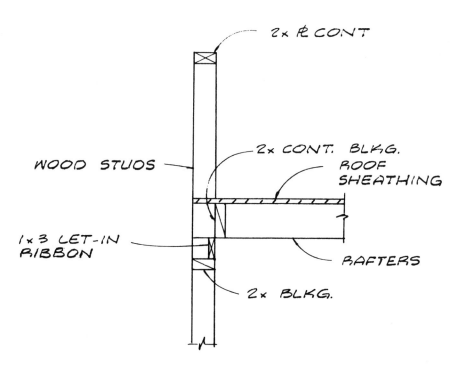

Detail 14. A section of a wood stud parapet wall and roof. The parapet is constructed by extending the wood studs above the top of the roof sheathing. The rafters and studs are blocked as shown to transfer the roof diaphragm stress into the wall. The rafters bear on the 1″ × 3″ let-in ribbon.

Notes ▪ Drawings ▪ Ideas

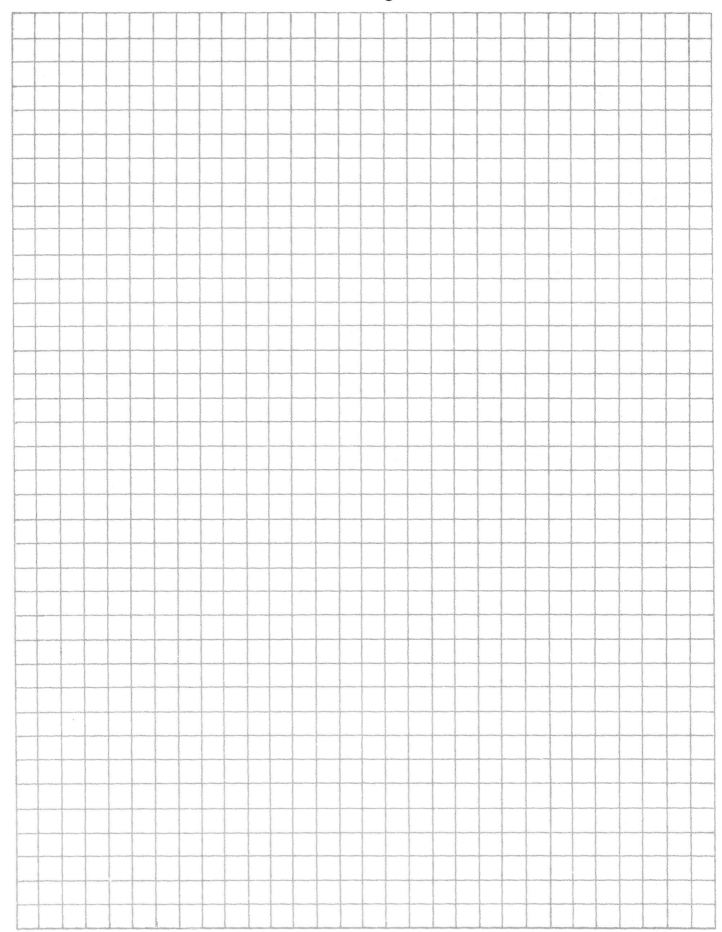

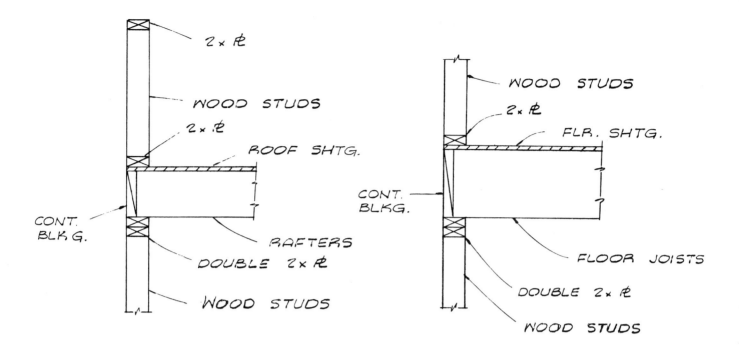

Detail 15. A section of a wood stud parapet wall and roof. The rafters bear on the wall double plates and are laterally braced by the continuous blocking.

Detail 16(a). A section of an exterior wood stud wall and floor joists. The joists bear on the wall double plates and are continuously blocked to complete the connection between the floor and the wall.

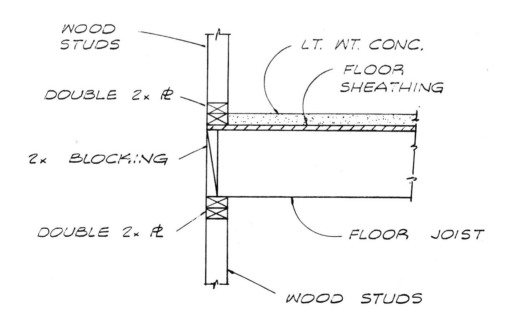

Detail 16(b). A section of an exterior wood stud wall and floor joists as shown in Detail 16(a). The floor sheathing is covered with light-weight concrete. The double plate of the stud wall on the floor is optional; a single plate may be used.

Notes ▪ Drawings ▪ Ideas

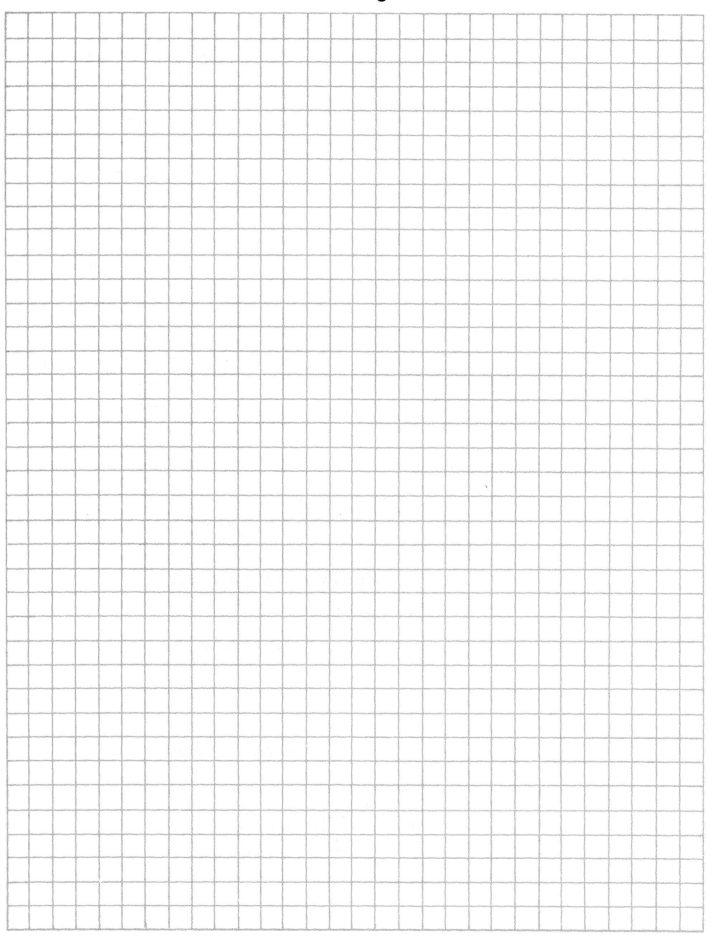

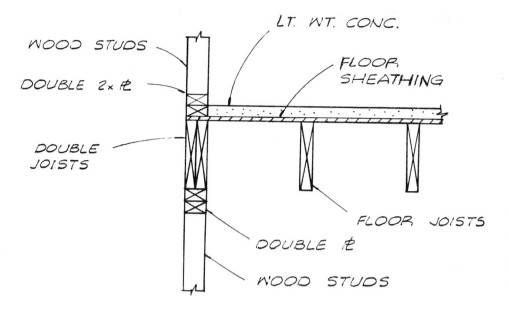

Detail 17. A section of an exterior wood stud wall, floor joists, and light-weight concrete over the floor sheathing. The joists span parallel to the wall. The double plate of the stud wall on the floor is optional; a single plate may be used.

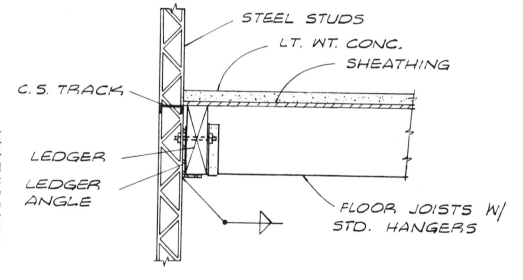

Detail 18(a). A section of an exterior steel stud wall, wood floor joists, and light-weight concrete over wood floor sheathing. A 4″ wide wood ledger is bolted to a continuous bent metal plate or ledger angle. The angle is welded to each stud to permit the transfer of lateral force from the floor diaphragm to the wall. The channel stud track between the studs acts as a strut in the wall.

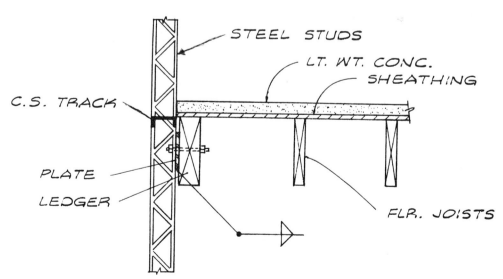

Detail 18(b). A section of an exterior steel stud wall, wood floor joists, and light-weight concrete over wood floor sheathing. The floor joists span parallel to the wall. A 4″ wide wood ledger is bolted to a continuous plate. The plate is welded to each stud to permit the transfer of lateral force from the floor diaphragm to the wall. The channel stud track between the studs acts as a strut in the wall.

Notes ▪ Drawings ▪ Ideas

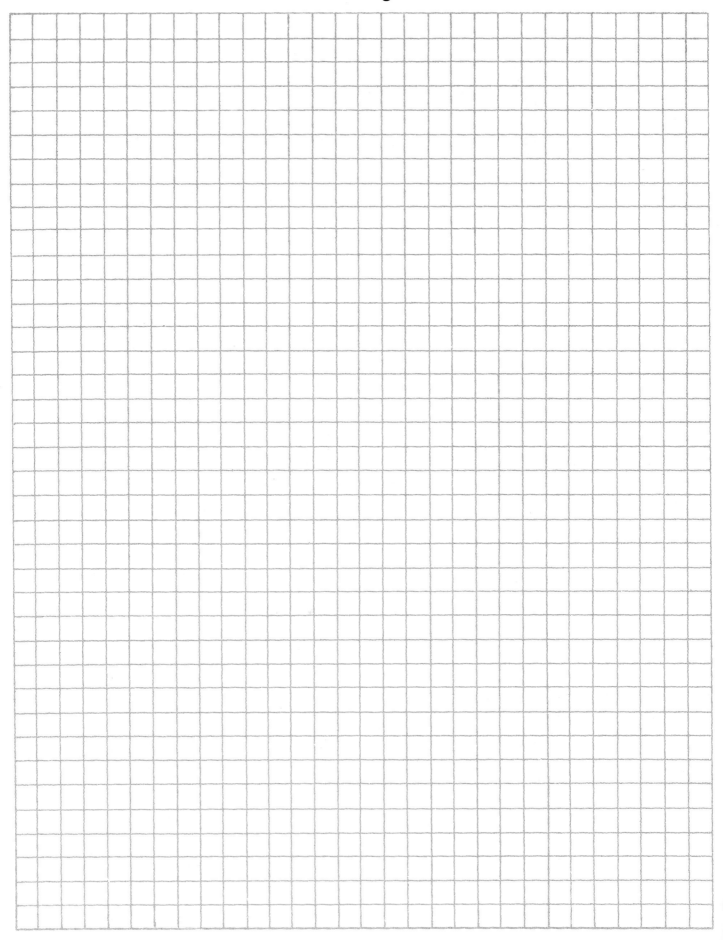

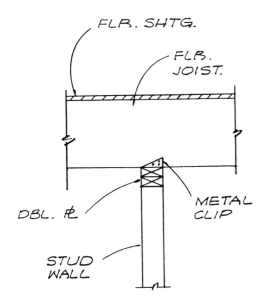

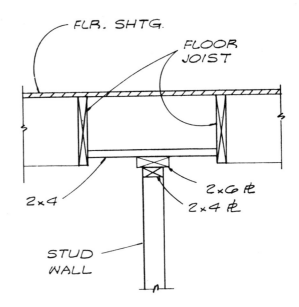

Detail 19(a). A section of a wood floor and floor joists which span parallel to a nonbearing wood stud partition wall. The top of the studs of the partition are connected to the floor joists as shown. The 2″ × 6″ continuous plate is nailed to the 2″ × 4″ members between the floor joists.

Detail 19(b). A section of a wood floor and floor joists that span perpendicular to a nonbearing wood stud partition wall. The double plate at the top of the studs is connected to the floor joists by toenails or with a sheet metal clip as shown.

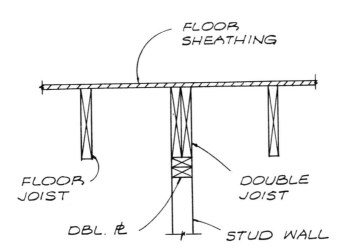

Detail 20. A section of a wood stud wall, floor sheathing, and floor joists. The double plate at the top of the wall is toenailed to the double floor joists.

Notes · Drawings · Ideas

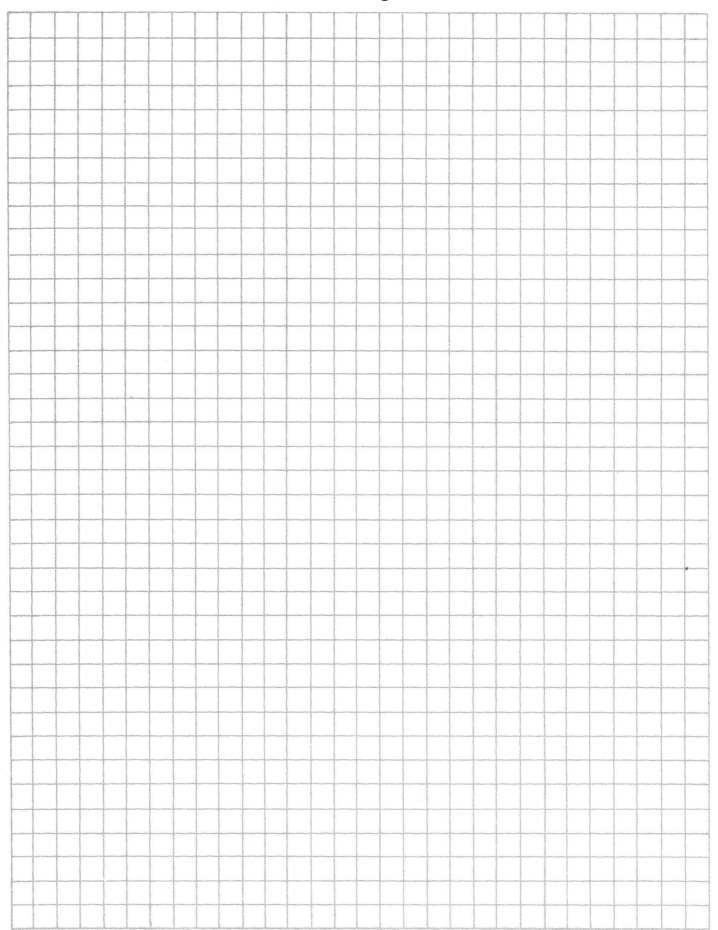

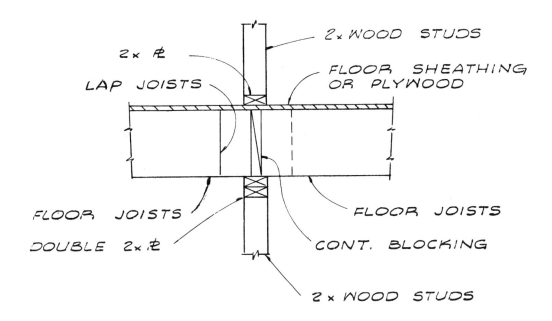

Detail 21. A section of an interior wood stud wall, floor sheathing and floor joists. The floor joists are lapped and nailed together and bear on the double plate at the top of the wall. The continuous blocking of the floor joists supports the wood stud wall and provides a means of transferring diaphragm loads from the floor to the walls.

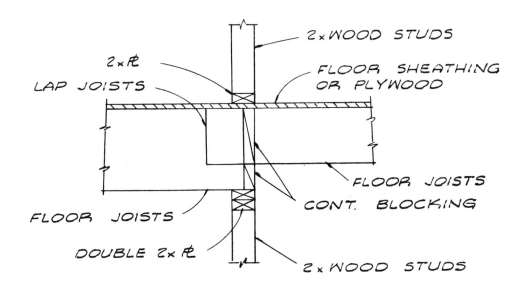

Detail 22. A section of an interior wood stud wall, floor sheathing, and floor joists. The wood floor joists on each side of the stud wall are unequal in depth. An extra continuous block is provided to support the smaller joist. The continuous blocking of the floor joists provides a means of transfer of the diaphragm load from the floor to the wall.

Notes ▪ Drawings ▪ Ideas

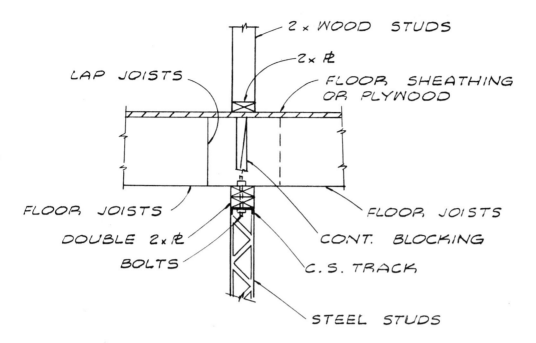

LAP JOISTS

2 x WOOD STUDS

2 x $\mathcal{R}$

FLOOR SHEATHING OR PLYWOOD

FLOOR JOISTS

DOUBLE 2 x $\mathcal{R}$

BOLTS

FLOOR JOISTS

CONT. BLOCKING

C. S. TRACK

STEEL STUDS

Detail 23(a). A section of an interior steel stud bearing wall, supporting wood floor joists and a wood stud wall. The floor joists are lapped and nailed together and bear on the double plate of the steel stud wall. The double 2″ × 4″ plate is bolted to the channel track at the top of the steel stud wall as shown. The continuous blocking provides a means of transfer of the diaphragm load to the steel stud wall.

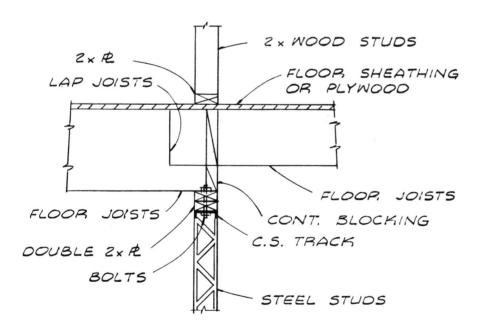

2 x $\mathcal{R}$

LAP JOISTS

2 x WOOD STUDS

FLOOR SHEATHING OR PLYWOOD

FLOOR JOISTS

CONT. BLOCKING

C.S. TRACK

FLOOR JOISTS

DOUBLE 2 x $\mathcal{R}$

BOLTS

STEEL STUDS

Detail 23(b). A section of an interior steel stud bearing wall, supporting wood floor joists and a wood stud wall. The floor joists are lapped and nailed together and bear on the double plate of the steel stud wall. The wood floor joists on each side of the steel stud wall are unequal in depth. An extra continuous block is provided to support the smaller joists. The double 2″ × 4″ plate is bolted to the channel track at the top of the steel stud wall as shown. The continuous blocking provides a means of transfer of the floor diaphragm load to the steel stud wall.

Notes ▪ Drawings ▪ Ideas

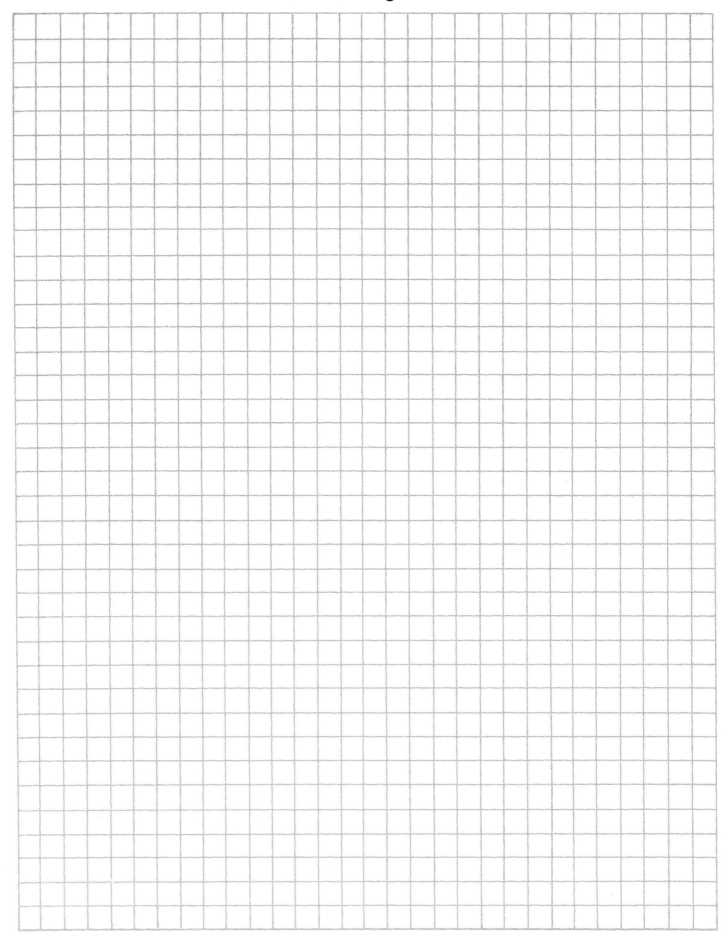

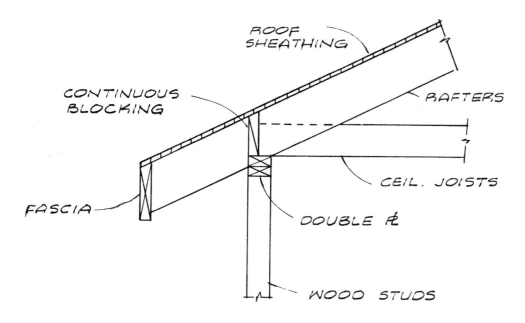

ROOF SHEATHING

CONTINUOUS BLOCKING

RAFTERS

CEIL. JOISTS

FASCIA

DOUBLE ℞

WOOD STUDS

Detail 24. A section of an exterior wood stud wall and a wood roof eave. The roof rafters and the ceiling joists are nailed to the double plate at the top of the wall. Continuous blocking is provided to transfer the roof diaphragm load to the wall.

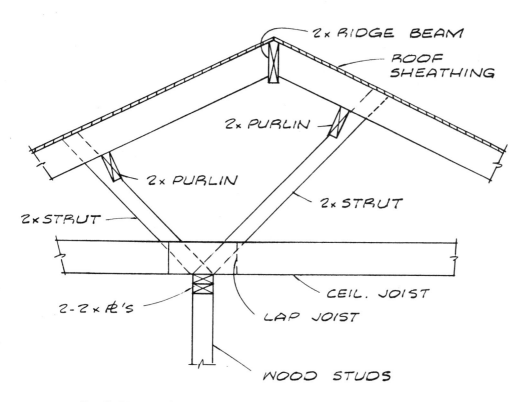

2× RIDGE BEAM

ROOF SHEATHING

2× PURLIN

2× PURLIN

2× STRUT

2× STRUT

CEIL. JOIST

2-2×℞'s

LAP JOIST

WOOD STUDS

Detail 25. A roof section supported by an interior wood stud wall. The 2″ wide struts supporting the roof to the wall should not slope more than 45° from the vertical. The wood struts are spaced at 4′0″ o.c. and the intermediate rafters are supported by the 2″ wide continuous purlins.

Notes · Drawings · Ideas

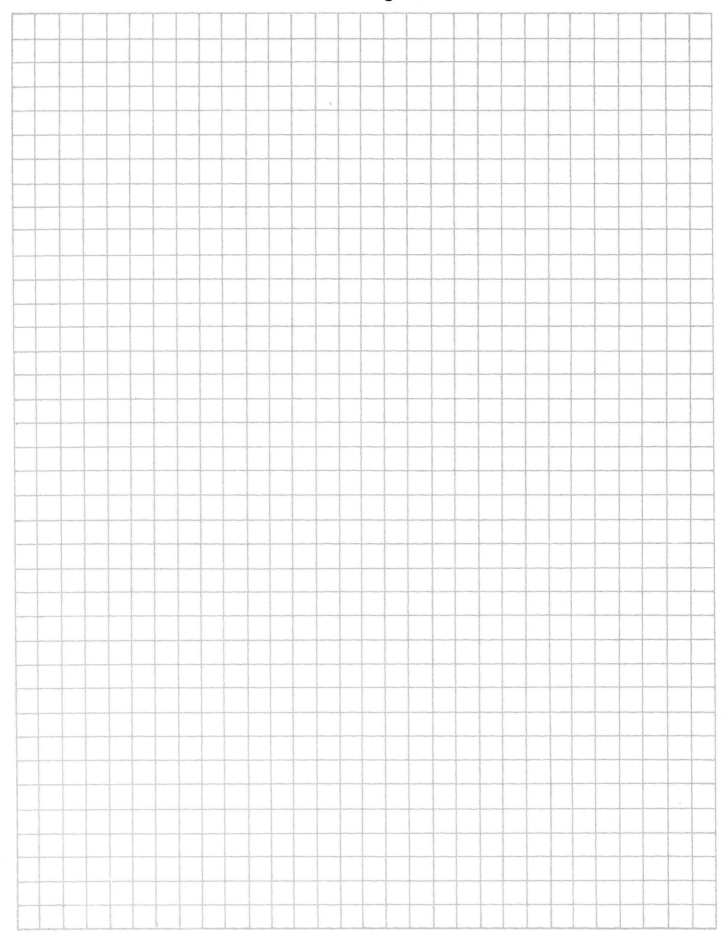

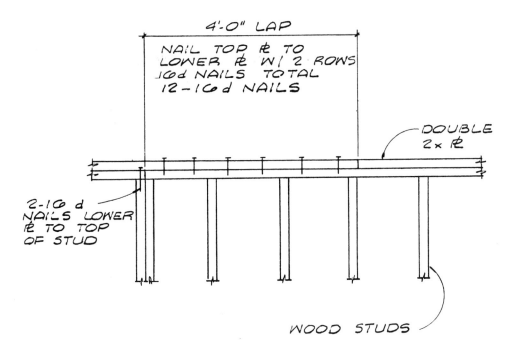

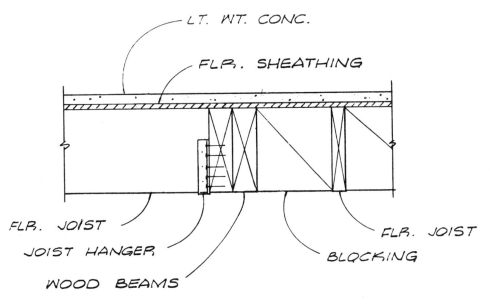

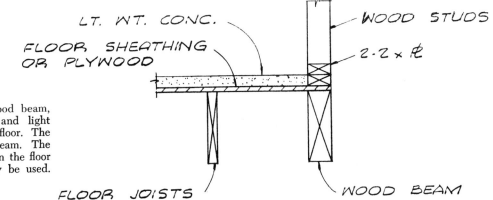

Detail 26. A lap splice of the top double plates of a wood stud wall. The width of the plates is equal to the width of the studs. The studs of the wall are tied together at the top with a double plate to transfer lateral force from a floor or roof diaphragm to the wall. The double plates must be properly lapped and nailed to make the total element effective in the transfer of lateral force.

Detail 27. A section of a laterally laminated wood beam, wood floor joists, and light-weight concrete on a wood floor. The joists are supported by the beam on the left side and span parallel to the beam on the right side. The beam is laterally laminated as shown in Detail 35(a).

Detail 28. A section of a wood beam, an exterior wood stud wall and light weight concrete on a wood floor. The joists span parallel to the beam. The double plate of the stud wall on the floor is optional; a single plate may be used.

37

Notes · Drawings · Ideas

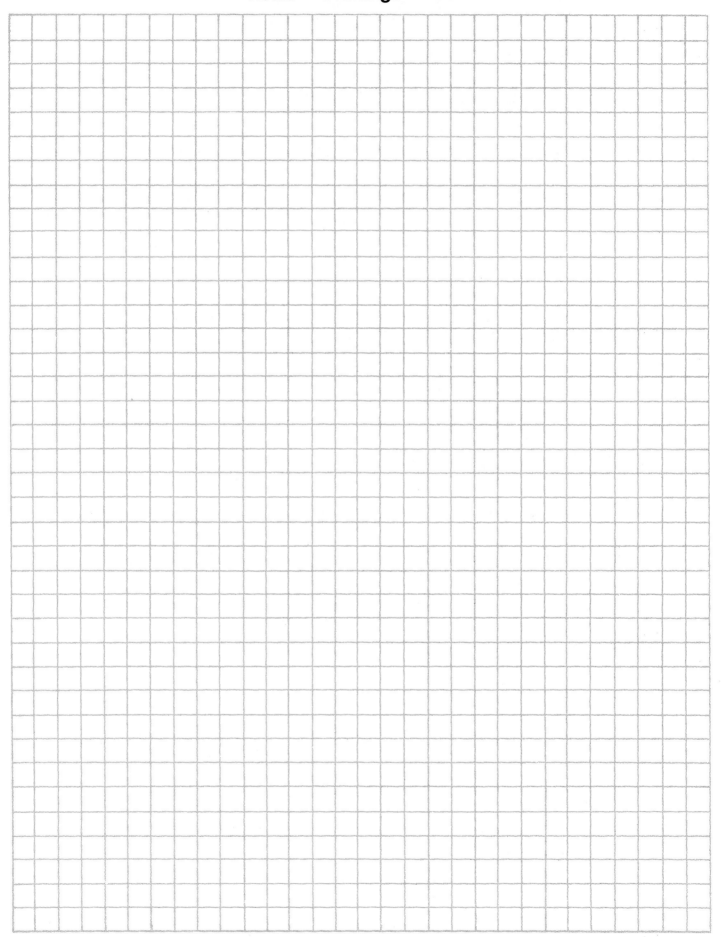

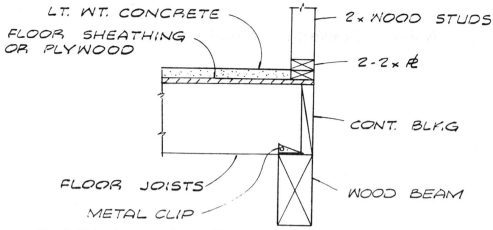

Detail 29(a). A section of a wood beam, an exterior wood stud wall, floor joists, and light-weight concrete on a wood floor. The floor joists are connected to the wood beam by toenailing or by a sheet metal clip as shown. The continuous blocking may be substituted with a continuous rim member provided that the floor joists have sufficient bearing area on the wood beam.

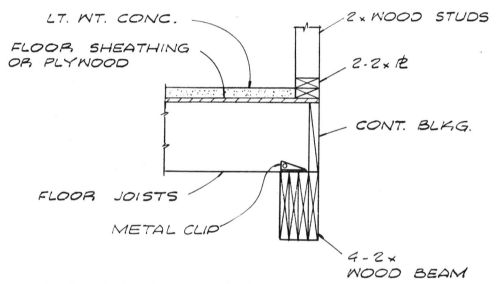

Detail 29(b). A section of a laterally laminated wood beam supporting an exterior wood stud wall, floor joists, and light-weight concrete on a wood floor. The floor joists are connected to the wood beam by toenails or by a sheet metal clip as shown. The continuous blocking may be substituted with a continuous rim member provided that the floor joists have sufficient bearing area on the wood beam. The wood beam is laminated as shown in Detail 35(a).

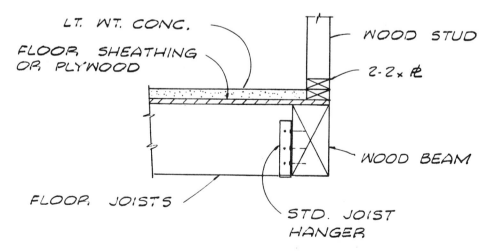

Detail 30. A section of a wood beam supporting an exterior wood stud wall, floor joists, and light-weight concrete on a wood floor. The floor joists are connected to the beam with standard joist hangers. The double plate of the stud wall on the floor is optional; a single plate may be used.

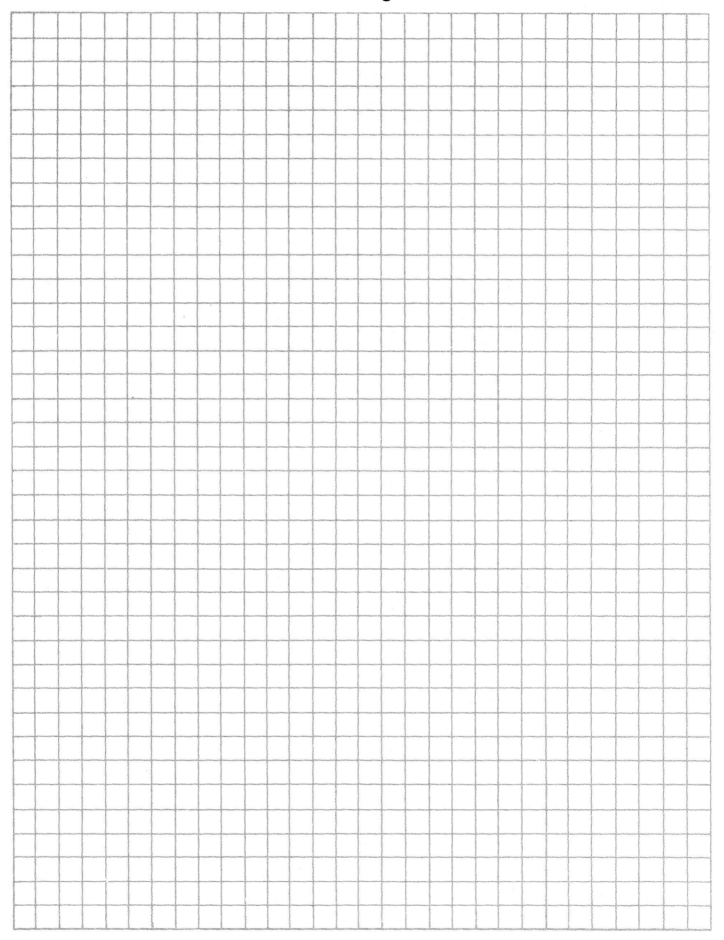

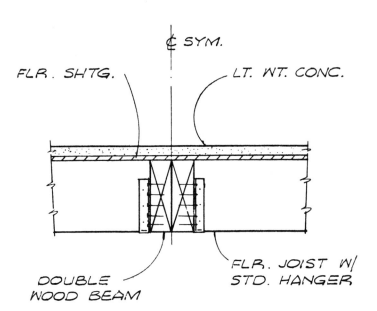

Detail 31. A section of a laterally laminated wood beam supporting floor joists and light-weight concrete on a wood floor. The wood beam is laminated as shown in Detail 35(a).

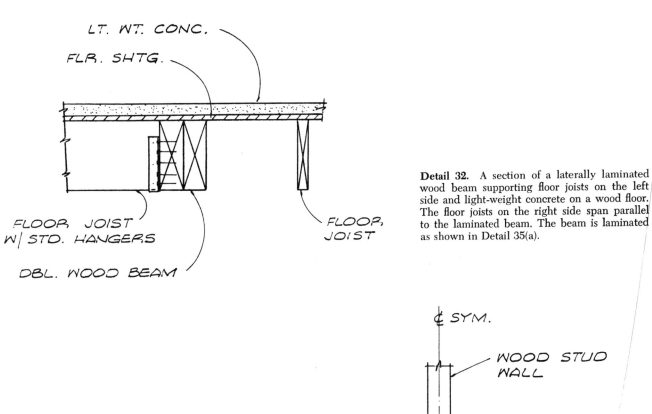

Detail 32. A section of a laterally laminated wood beam supporting floor joists on the left side and light-weight concrete on a wood floor. The floor joists on the right side span parallel to the laminated beam. The beam is laminated as shown in Detail 35(a).

Detail 33. A section of a laterally laminated wood beam supporting floor joists, a wood stud wall, and light-weight concrete on a wood floor. The beam is laminated as shown in Detail 35(a). The double plate of the stud wall on the floor is optional; a single plate may be used.

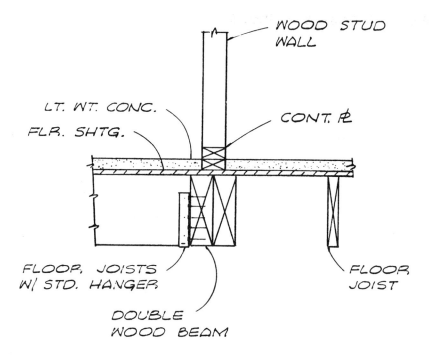

WOOD STUD WALL

LT. WT. CONC.

FLR. SHTG.

CONT. ℔

FLOOR JOISTS W/ STD. HANGER

FLOOR JOIST

DOUBLE WOOD BEAM

Detail 34. A section of a laterally laminated wood beam supporting floor joists, a wood stud wall, and light-weight concrete on a wood floor. The floor joists on the right side span parallel to the laminated beam. The beam is laminated as shown in Detail 35(a). The double plate of the stud wall on the floor is optional; a single plate may be used.

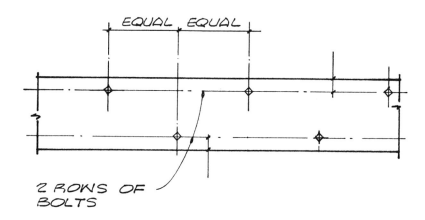

EQUAL EQUAL

2 ROWS OF BOLTS

Detail 35(a). An elevation of a laterally laminated wood beam showing the bolts and spacing required. See Detail 35(b).

3 OR MORE 2 x OR 2 - 4 x WOOD MEMBERS

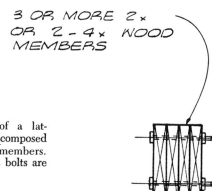

Detail 35(b). A section of a laterally laminated wood beam composed of 2″ wide or 4″ wide members. The size and spacing of the bolts are determined by calculation.

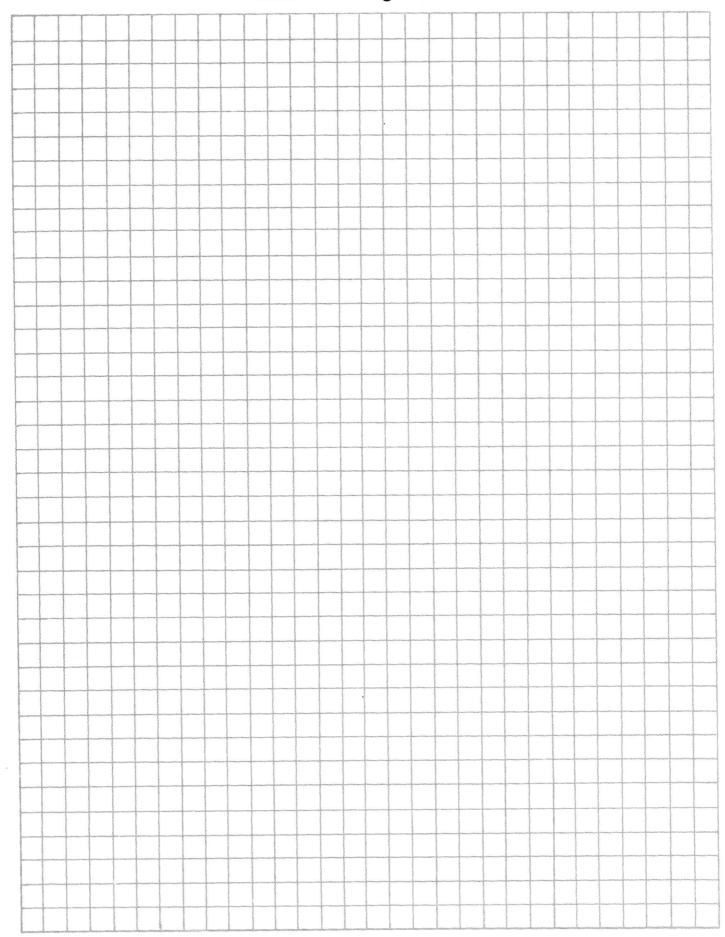

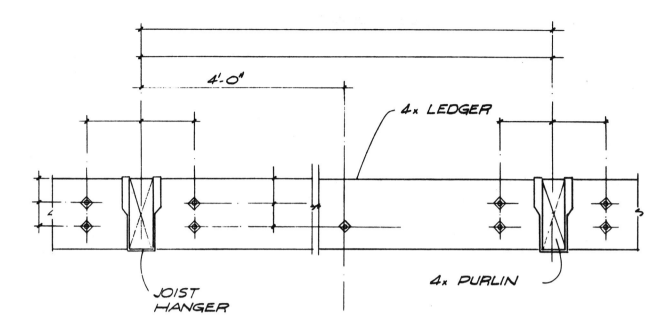

Detail 36. An elevation of a 4″ wide wood ledger and bolts. The ledger may be bolted to a masonry or concrete wall. The size and spacing of the bolts are determined by calculation. The purlins are also shown in Detail 9(a).

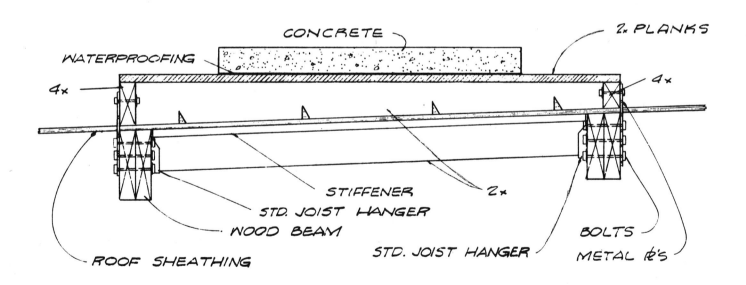

Detail 37. A section of a wood platform used to support mechanical equipment on a plywood panelized roof. See Detail 9(a). The platform is supported by and connected to the roof beams with metal straps bolted as shown. The connections should be capable of resisting lateral loads caused by wind or seismic forces. The concrete slab on the platform serves to dampen vibrational forces caused by the operation of mechanical equipment.

Notes ▪ Drawings ▪ Ideas

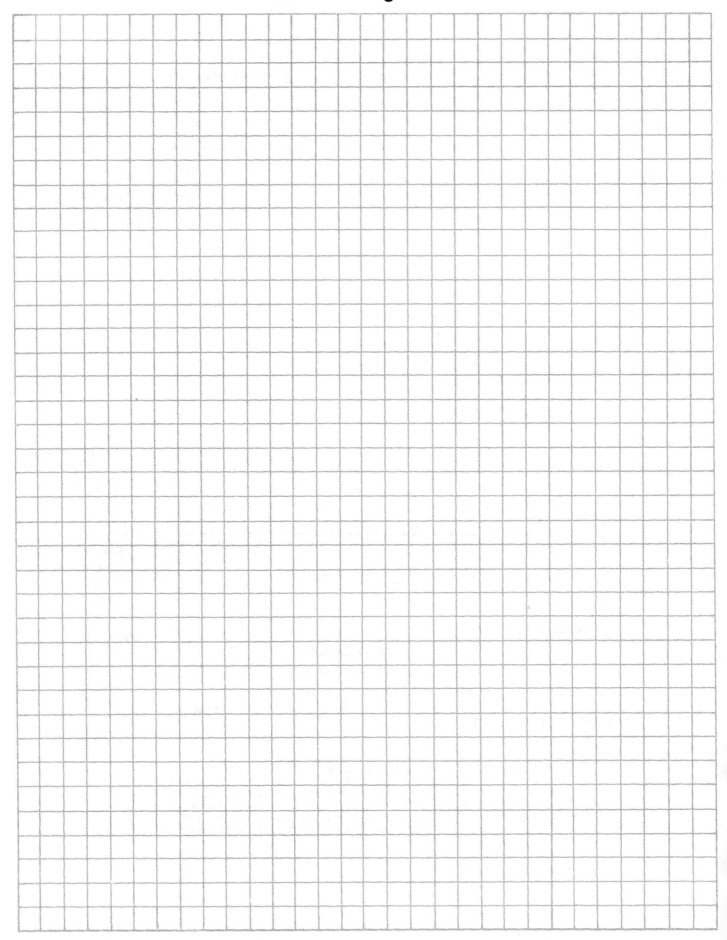

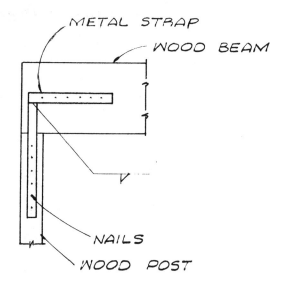

Detail 38(a). An end connection of a wood beam to a wood post. The connection is made with metal side plates and nails on each side of the post and beam.

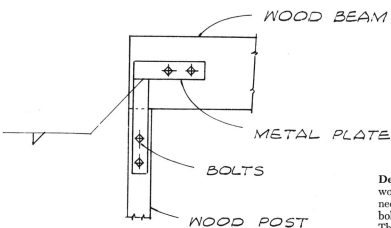

Detail 38(b). An end connection of a wood beam to a wood post. The connection is made with metal side plates and bolts on each side of the post and beam. The size and spacing of the bolts are determined by calculation.

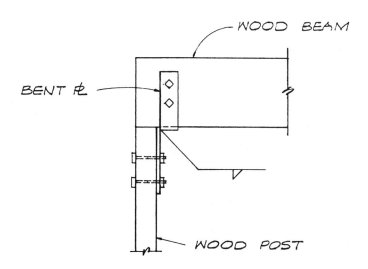

Detail 39. An end connection of a wood beam to a wood post. The method of the connection allows the beam and the post to be of different widths.

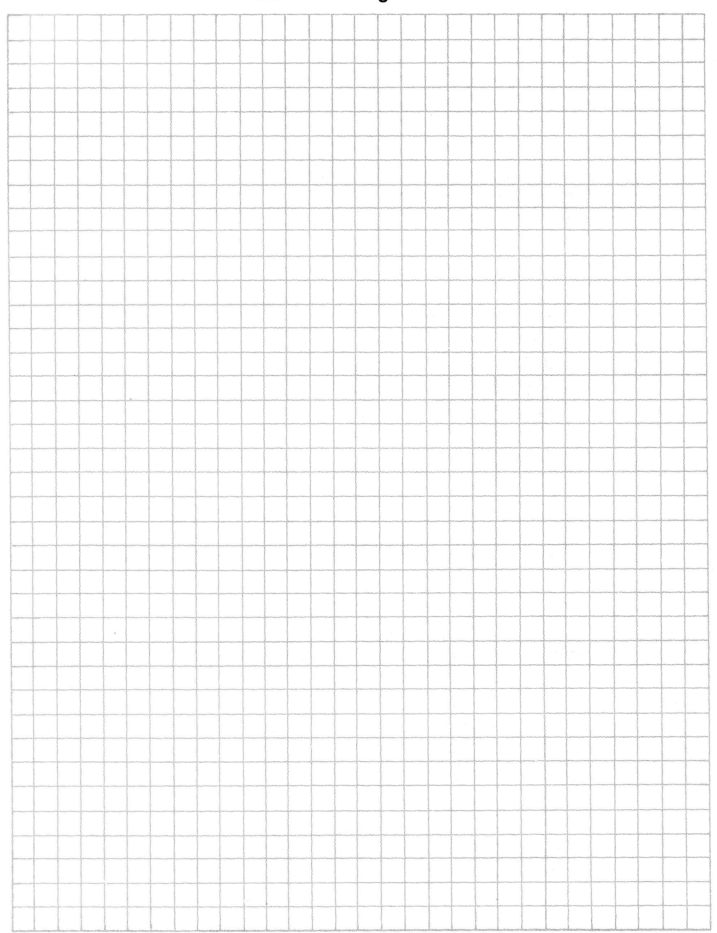

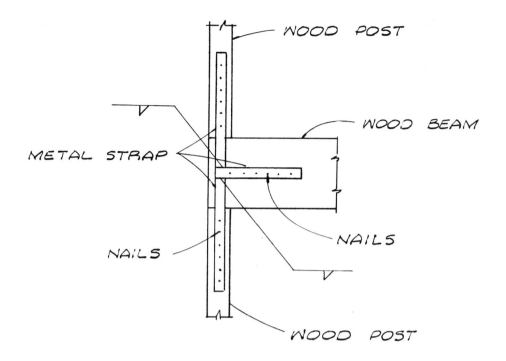

Detail 40(a). An end connection of a wood beam to wood posts. The connection is made with metal side plates and nails to each side of the beam and the posts.

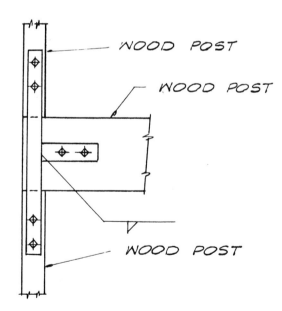

Detail 40(b). An end connection of a wood beam to wood posts. The connection is made with metal side plates and bolts through each side of the beam and posts.

Notes · Drawings · Ideas

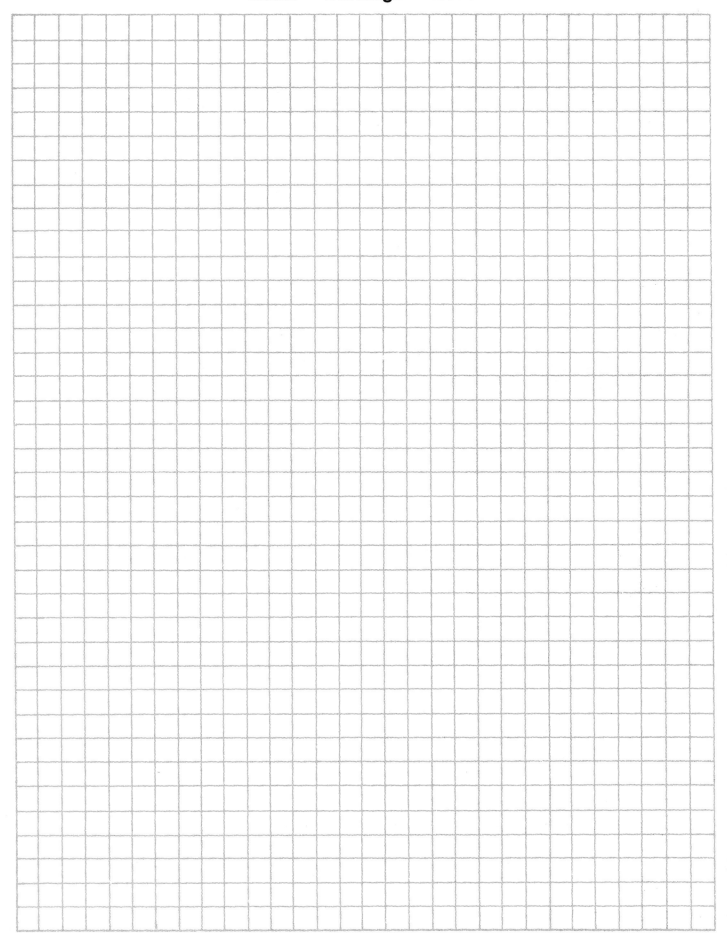

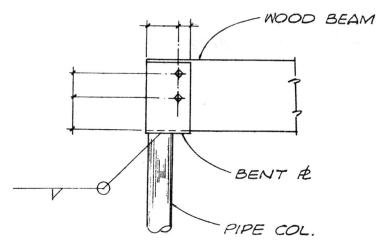

Detail 41(a). An end connection of a wood beam to a steel pipe column. The U-shaped metal plate is bolted through the wood beam and welded to the top of the pipe column.

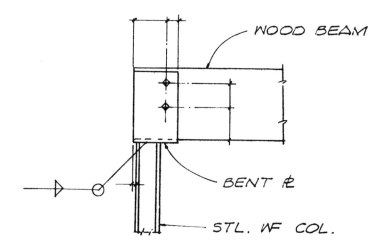

Detail 41(b). An end connection of a wood beam to a wide flange steel column. The U-shaped metal plate is bolted through the wood beam and welded to the top of the wide flange column.

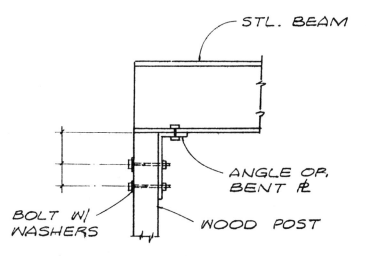

Detail 42. An end connection of a steel beam to a wood post. The vertical leg of the connection angle is bolted to the post with two bolts as shown. The horizontal leg of the connection angle is bolted to the bottom flange of the steel beam with two bolts, one bolt on each side of the beam web.

Notes ▪ Drawings ▪ Ideas

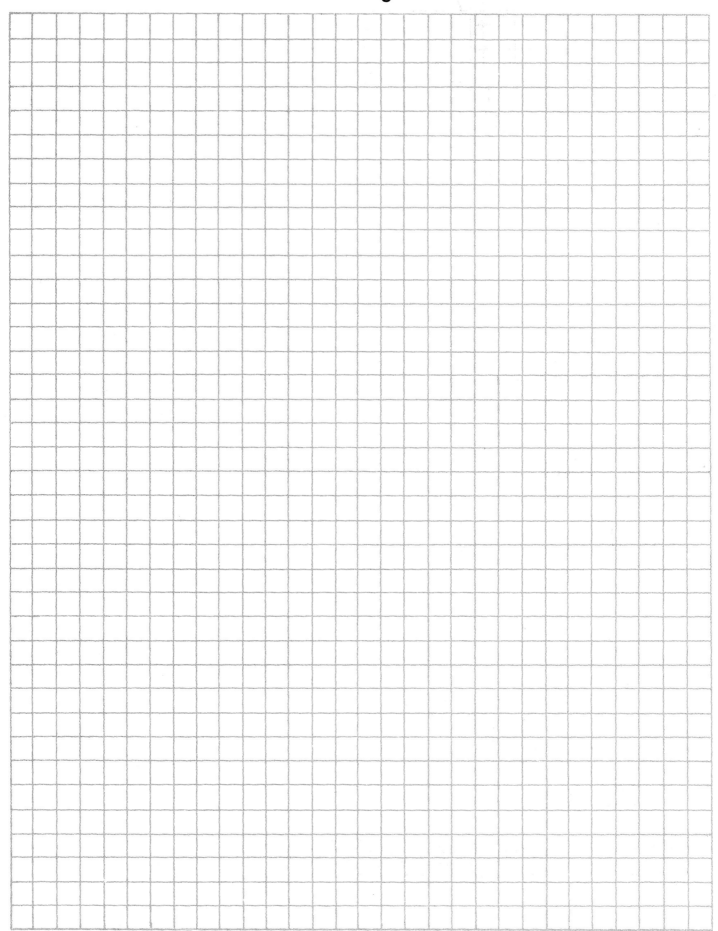

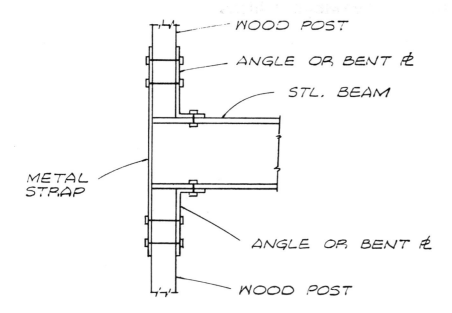

Detail 43. An end connection of a steel beam to wood posts. The vertical legs of the connection angles at the top and bottom of the steel beam are bolted to the posts with two bolts as shown. The horizontal legs of the connection angles are bolted to the top and bottom flanges of the steel beam with two bolts, one bolt on each side of the beam web. The metal strap on the face of the posts connects the top post to the bottom post.

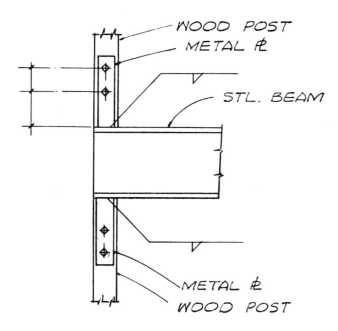

Detail 44. An end connection of a steel beam to wood posts. The plates on each side of the posts are welded to the top and bottom flanges of the beam.

Notes ▪ Drawings ▪ Ideas

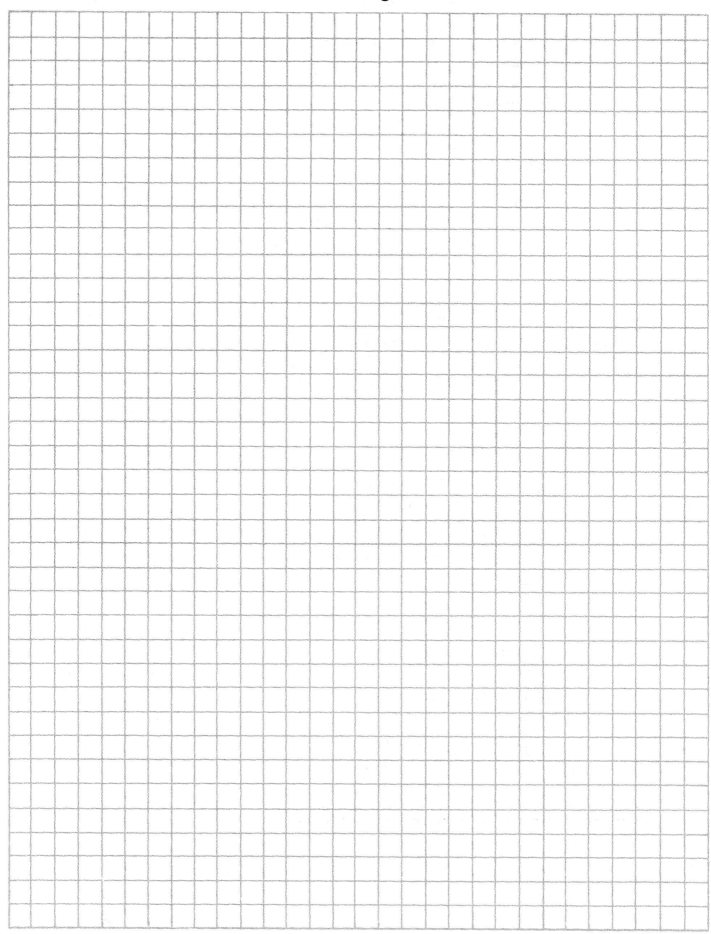

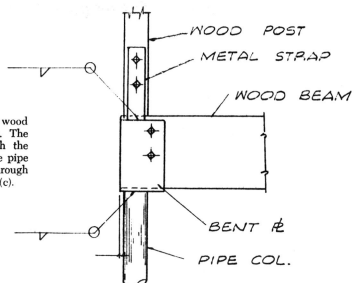

WOOD POST

METAL STRAP

WOOD BEAM

BENT ℔

PIPE COL.

Detail 45(a). An end connection of a wood beam and post to a steel pipe column. The U-shaped metal plate is bolted through the wood beam and welded to the top of the pipe column. The metal plates are bolted through each side of the wood post. See Detail 45(c).

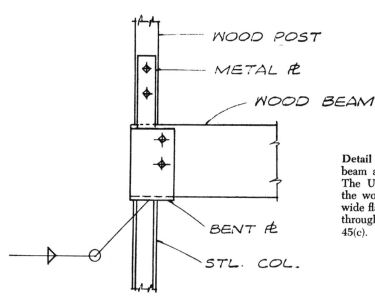

WOOD POST

METAL ℔

WOOD BEAM

BENT ℔

STL. COL.

Detail 45(b). An end connection of a wood beam and post to a wide flange steel column. The U-shaped metal plate is bolted through the wood beam and welded to the top of the wide flange column. The metal plates are bolted through each side of the wood post. See Detail 45(c).

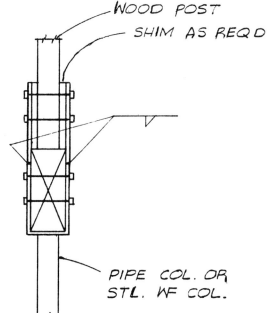

WOOD POST

SHIM AS REQD

PIPE COL. OR STL. WF COL.

Detail 45(c). A section of Details 45(a) and 55. Wood shim plates are added between the metal side plates and the post.

Notes ▪ Drawings ▪ Ideas

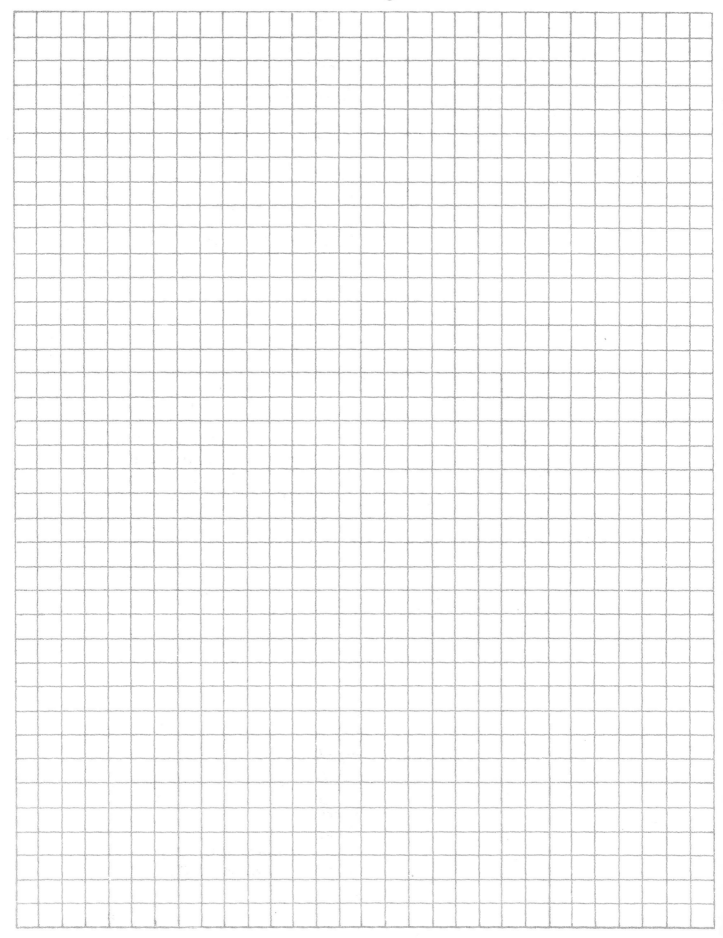

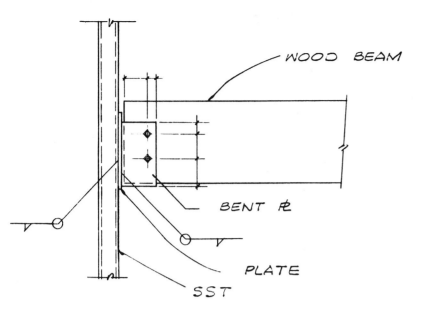

WOOD BEAM

BENT ℞

PLATE

SST

Detail 46. An end connection of a wood beam to a continuous structural steel tube column. The plate at the face of the column serves to adapt the width of the beam to the width of the column. The U-shaped metal plate is bolted through the beam and welded to the plate on the face of the column.

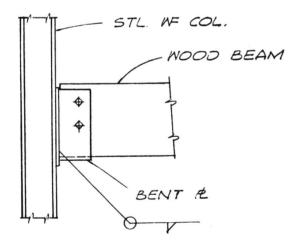

STL. WF COL.

WOOD BEAM

BENT ℞

Detail 47. An end connection of a wood beam to a continuous wide-flange steel column. The metal plate at the face of the column serves to adapt the width of the beam to the width of the column. The U-shaped metal plate is bolted through the beam and welded to the plate on the face of the column.

Notes ▪ Drawings ▪ Ideas

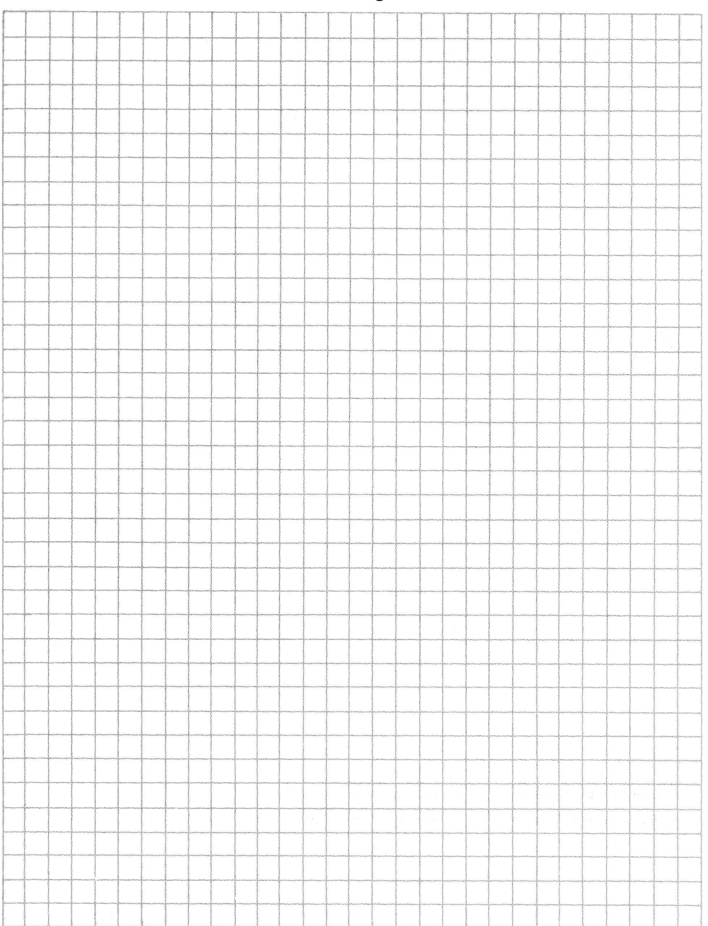

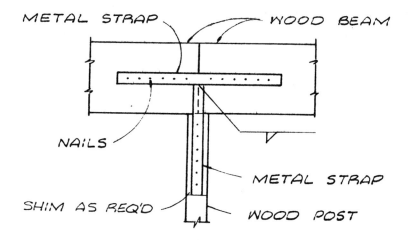

Detail 48(a). A wood beam and post connection. The metal straps are nailed to each side of the beam and post. The beams should set on the post to allow sufficient bearing area between the post and the beam. Wood shim plates are added to the sides of the post when the width of the beam is greater than the width of the post.

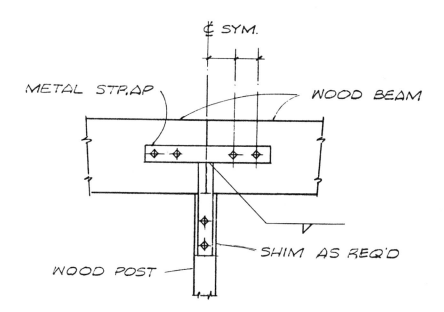

Detail 48(b). A wood beam and post connection. The metal straps are bolted through each side of the beams and post. The beams should set on the post to allow sufficient bearing area between the post and the beam. Wood shim plates are added to the sides of the post when the width of the beam is greater than the width of the post.

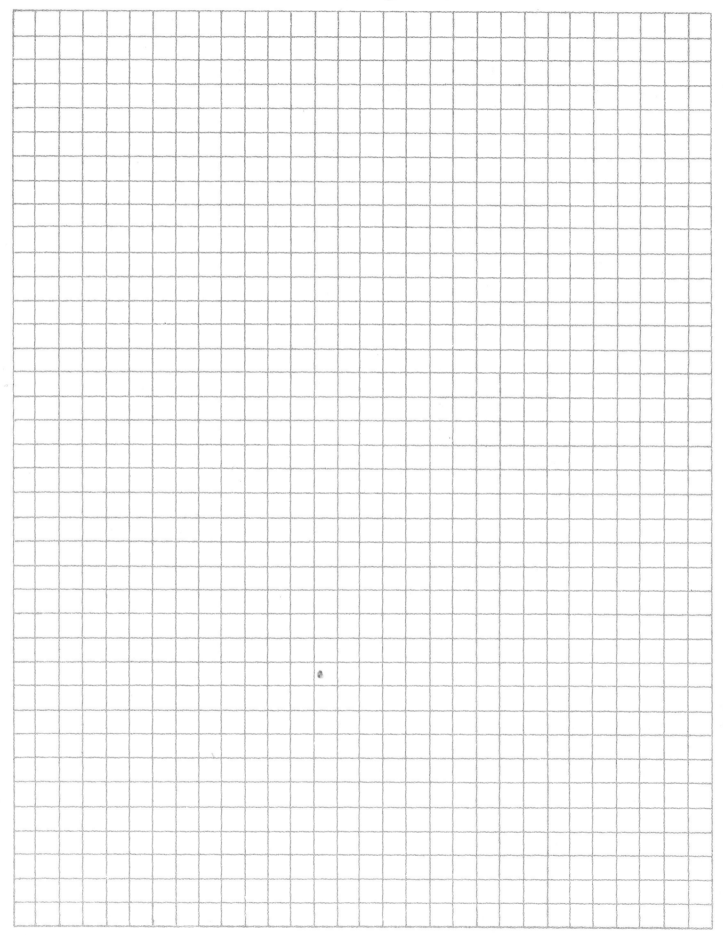

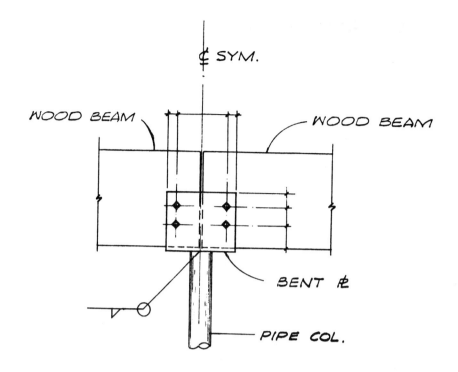

Detail 49(a). A connection of wood beams to a steel pipe column. The U-shaped metal plate is bolted through the beams and welded to the top of the pipe column.

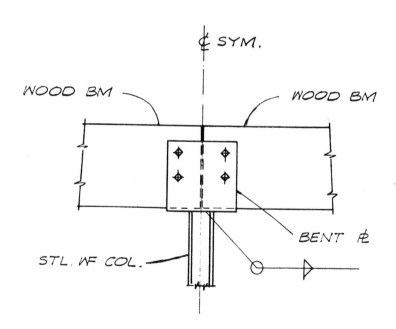

Detail 49(b). A connection of wood beams to a wide flange steel column. The U-shaped metal plate is bolted through the beams and welded to the top of the wide flange column.

Notes · Drawings · Ideas

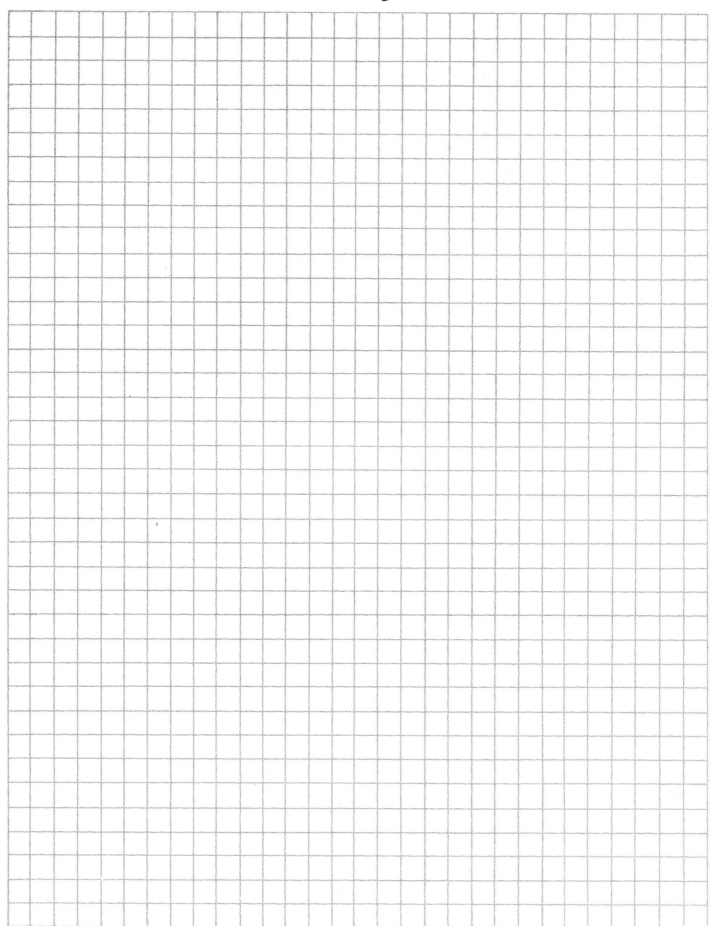

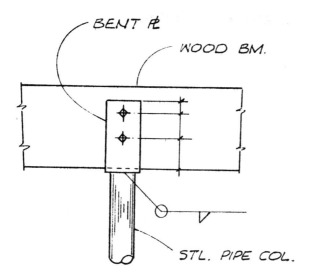

Detail 50(a). A connection of a cantilevered or continuous wood beam to a steel pipe column. The U-shaped metal plate is bolted through the beam and welded to the top of the pipe column.

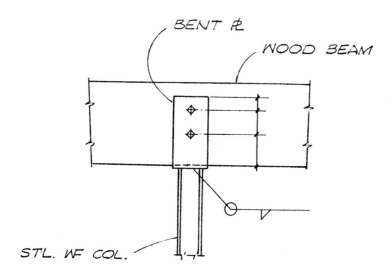

Detail 50(b). A connection of a cantilevered or continuous wood beam to a wide flange steel column. The U-shaped metal plate is bolted through the beam and welded to the top of the wide flange column.

Notes ▪ Drawings ▪ Ideas

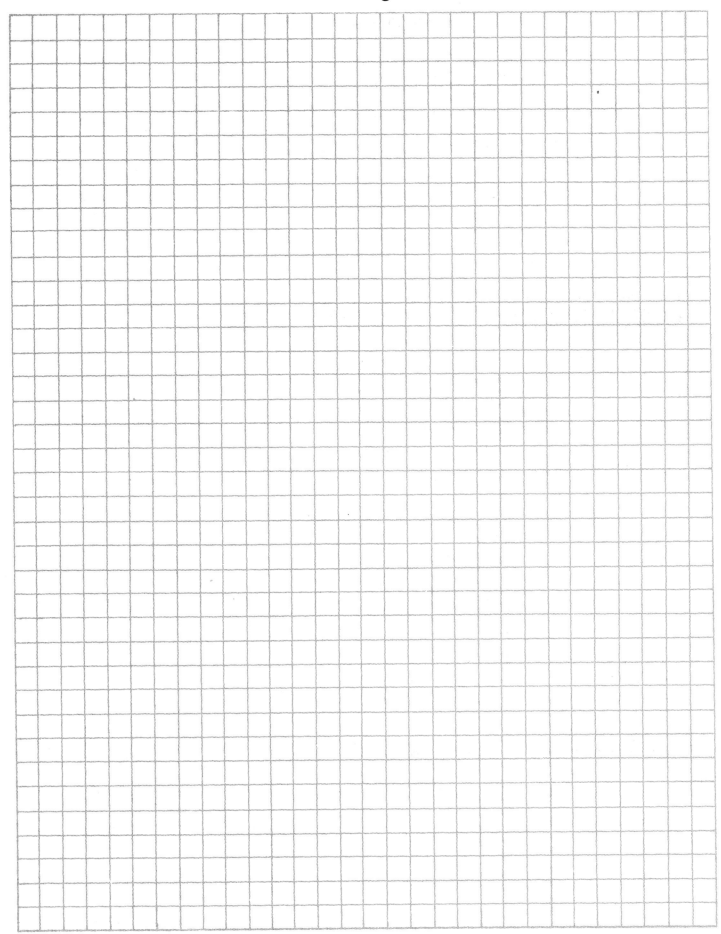

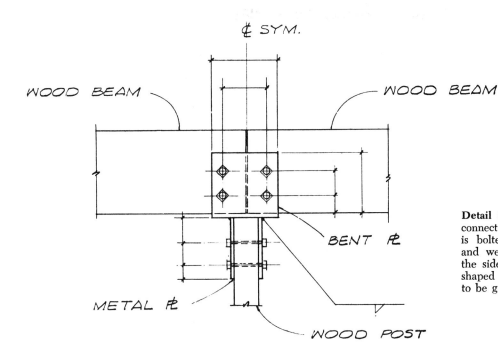

¢ SYM.

WOOD BEAM

WOOD BEAM

BENT ℞

METAL ℞

WOOD POST

Detail 51. A wood beam and post connection. The U-shaped metal plate is bolted through the wood beams and welded to the metal plates on the sides of the wood post. The U-shaped plate allows the beam width to be greater than the post width.

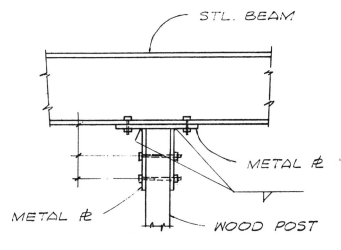

STL. BEAM

METAL ℞

METAL ℞

WOOD POST

Detail 52. A connection of a wood post supporting a cantilevered or continuous steel beam. The horizontal plate at the top of the post is bolted to the bottom flange of the steel beam with two bolts on each side of the beam web. The metal plates bolted through each side of the post are welded to the horizontal plate as shown.

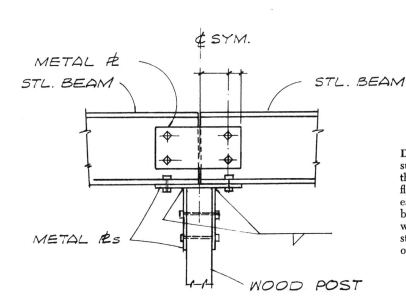

¢ SYM.

METAL ℞
STL. BEAM

STL. BEAM

METAL ℞s

WOOD POST

Detail 53. A connection of a wood post supporting steel beams. The horizontal plate at the top of the post is bolted to the bottom flange of the steel beams with two bolts on each side of the beam web. The metal plates bolted through each side of the post are welded to the horizontal plate as shown. The steel beams are connected by plates bolted on each side of the beam web.

Notes · Drawings · Ideas

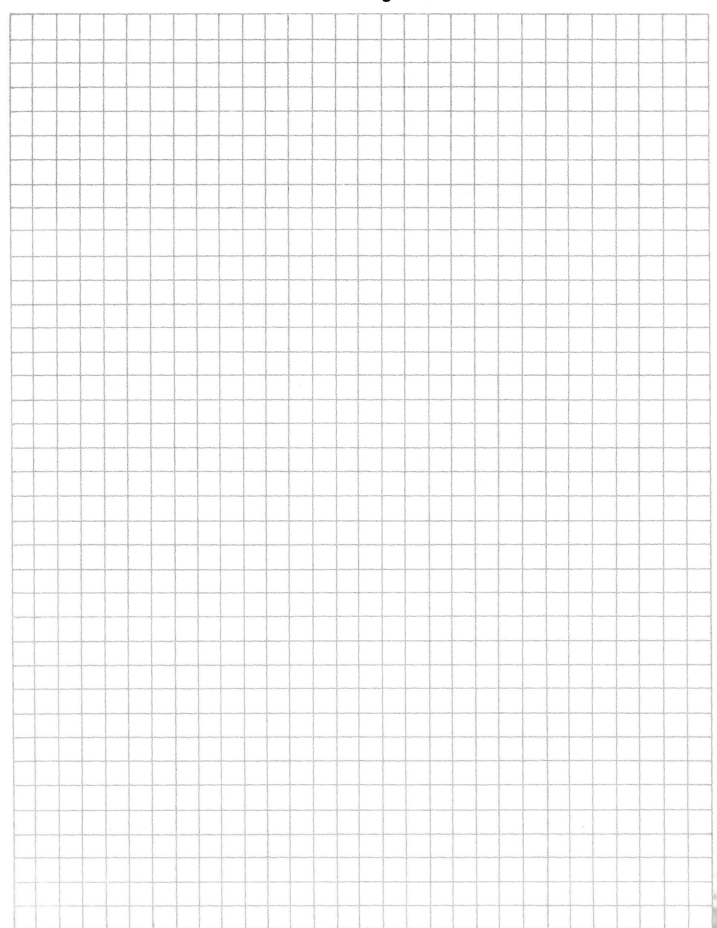

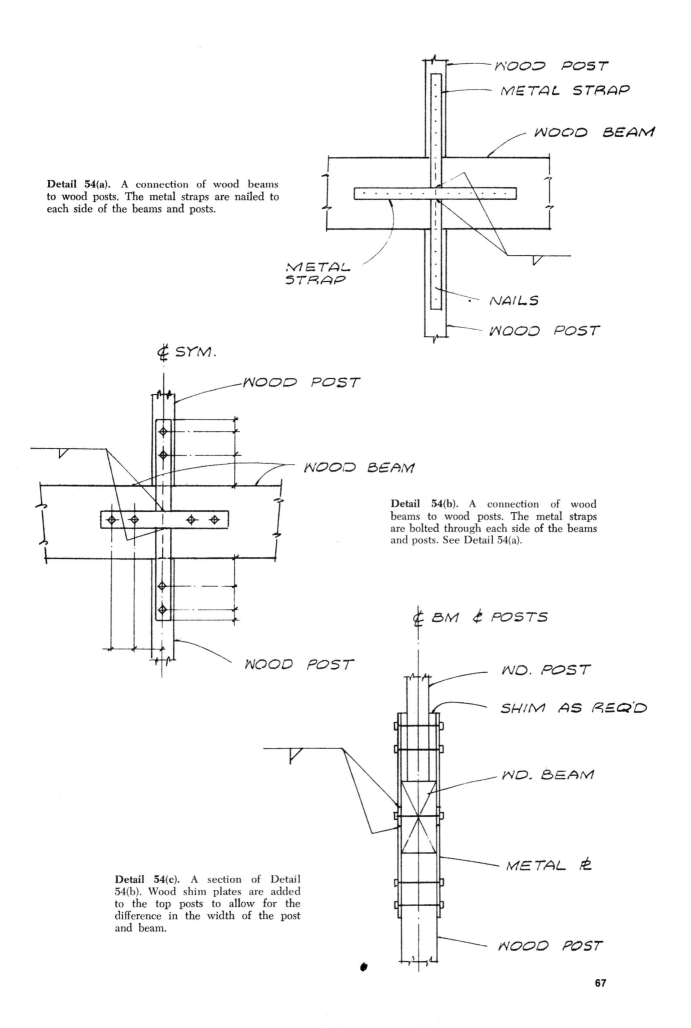

Detail 54(a). A connection of wood beams to wood posts. The metal straps are nailed to each side of the beams and posts.

WOOD POST

METAL STRAP

WOOD BEAM

METAL STRAP

NAILS

WOOD POST

℄ SYM.

WOOD POST

WOOD BEAM

WOOD POST

Detail 54(b). A connection of wood beams to wood posts. The metal straps are bolted through each side of the beams and posts. See Detail 54(a).

℄ BM ℄ POSTS

WD. POST

SHIM AS REQ'D

WD. BEAM

METAL ℄

WOOD POST

Detail 54(c). A section of Detail 54(b). Wood shim plates are added to the top posts to allow for the difference in the width of the post and beam.

Notes · Drawings · Ideas

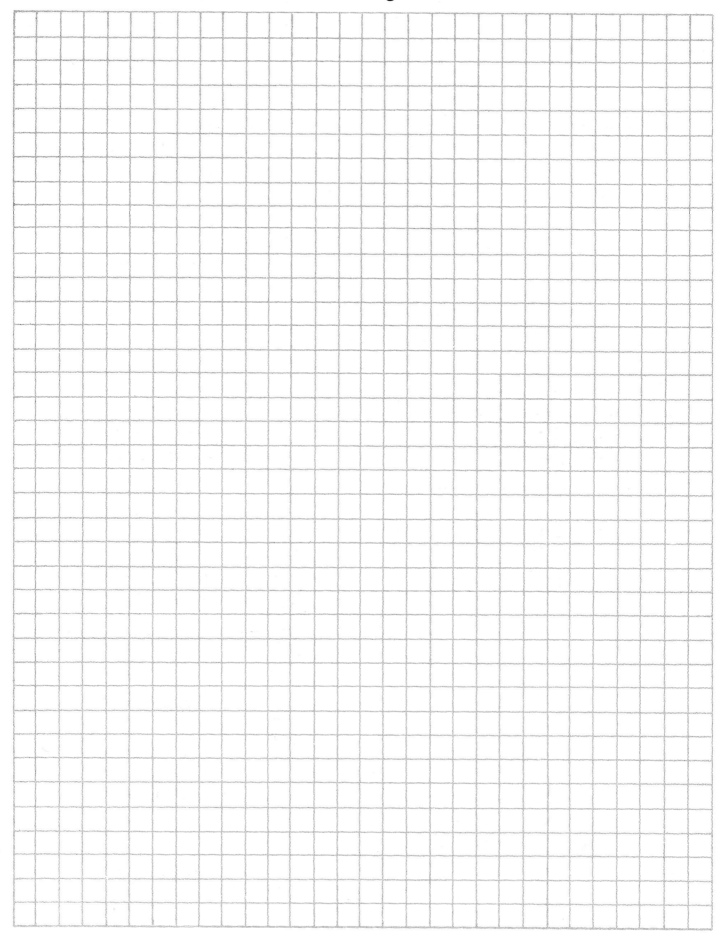

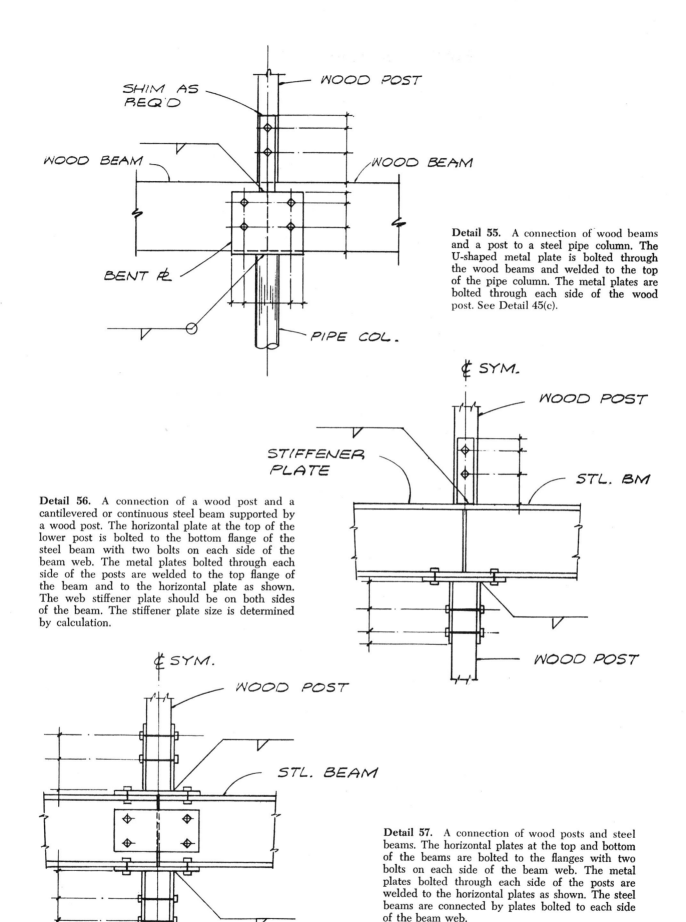

Detail 55. A connection of wood beams and a post to a steel pipe column. The U-shaped metal plate is bolted through the wood beams and welded to the top of the pipe column. The metal plates are bolted through each side of the wood post. See Detail 45(c).

SHIM AS REQ'D

WOOD POST

WOOD BEAM

WOOD BEAM

BENT ℞

PIPE COL.

€ SYM.

WOOD POST

STIFFENER PLATE

STL. BM

WOOD POST

Detail 56. A connection of a wood post and a cantilevered or continuous steel beam supported by a wood post. The horizontal plate at the top of the lower post is bolted to the bottom flange of the steel beam with two bolts on each side of the beam web. The metal plates bolted through each side of the posts are welded to the top flange of the beam and to the horizontal plate as shown. The web stiffener plate should be on both sides of the beam. The stiffener plate size is determined by calculation.

€ SYM.

WOOD POST

STL. BEAM

WOOD POST

Detail 57. A connection of wood posts and steel beams. The horizontal plates at the top and bottom of the beams are bolted to the flanges with two bolts on each side of the beam web. The metal plates bolted through each side of the posts are welded to the horizontal plates as shown. The steel beams are connected by plates bolted to each side of the beam web.

69

Notes ▪ Drawings ▪ Ideas

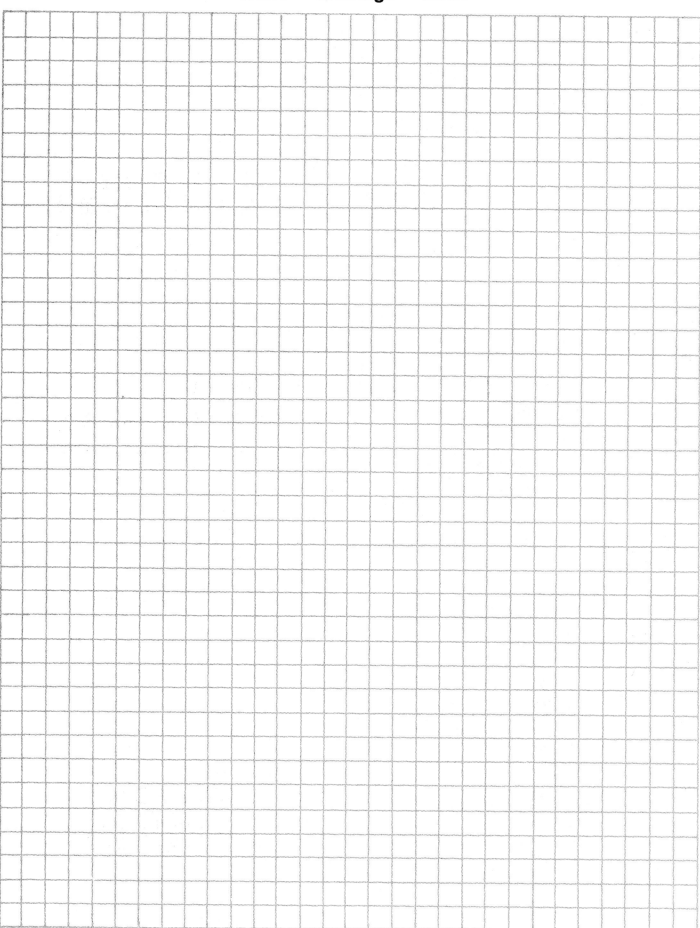

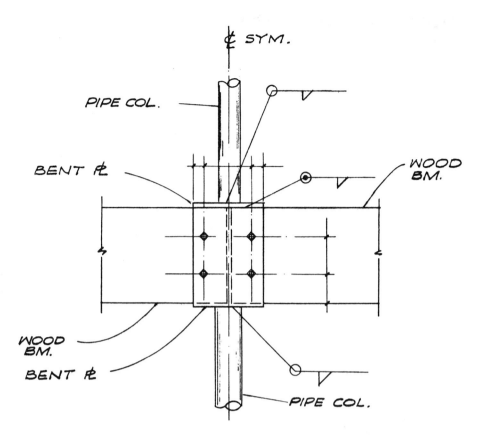

Detail 58(a). A connection of wood beams and steel pipe columns. The L-shaped metal plates are bolted through the beams and welded to the top and bottom of the pipe columns as shown. See Detail 58(b).

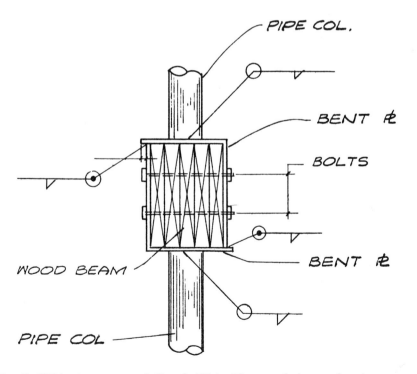

Detail 58(b). A section of Detail 58(a). The wood beam that is shown is composed of laterally laminated 2″ wide members. See Detail 35(b). The L-shaped side plates bear on each other to transfer the vertical column load if the wood beams compress or shrink away from the metal plates.

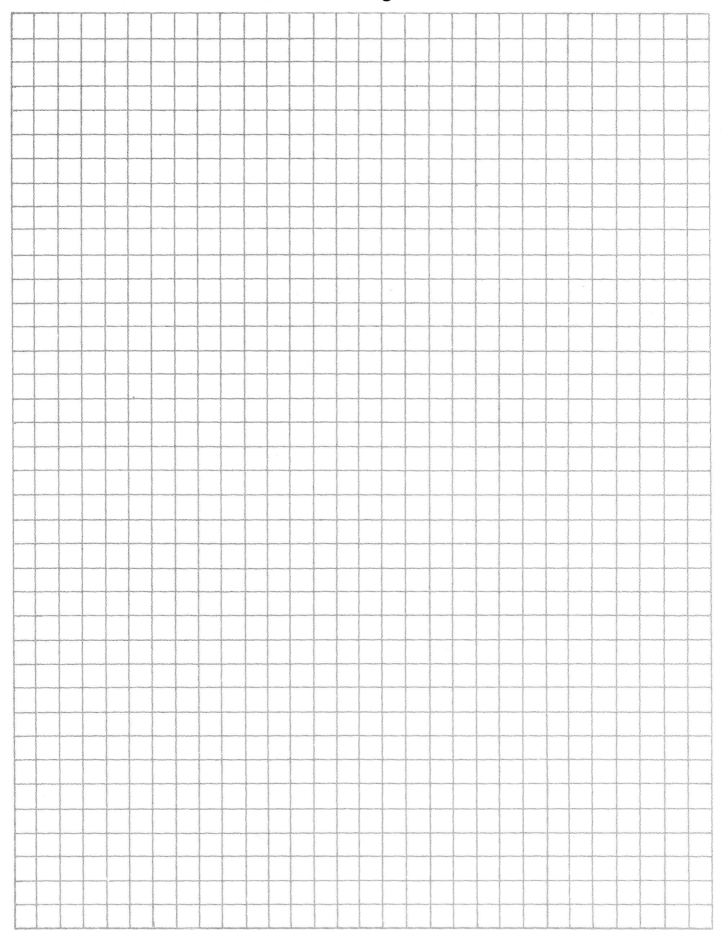

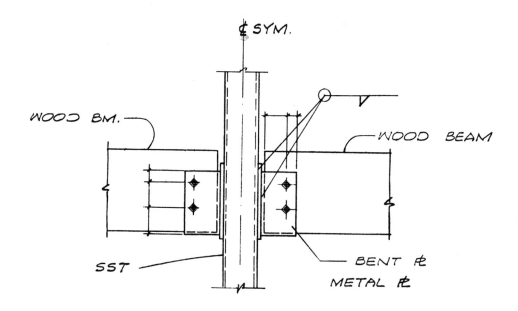

Detail 59. Connection of wood beams to a continuous structural steel tube column. The metal plates at each face of the column serve to adapt the width of the beams to the width of the column. The U-shaped metal plates are bolted through the beams and welded to the face of the column plates.

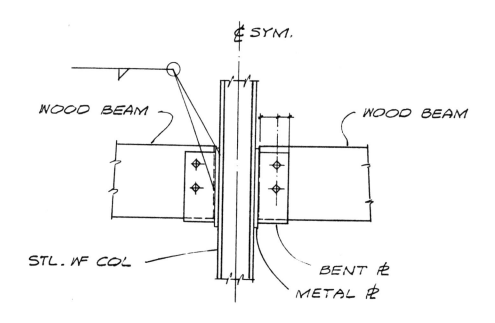

Detail 60. A connection of wood beams to a continuous wide flange steel column. The metal plates at each face of the column serve to adapt the width of the beams to the width of the column. The U-shaped metal plates are bolted through the beams and welded to the face of the column plates.

Notes · Drawings · Ideas

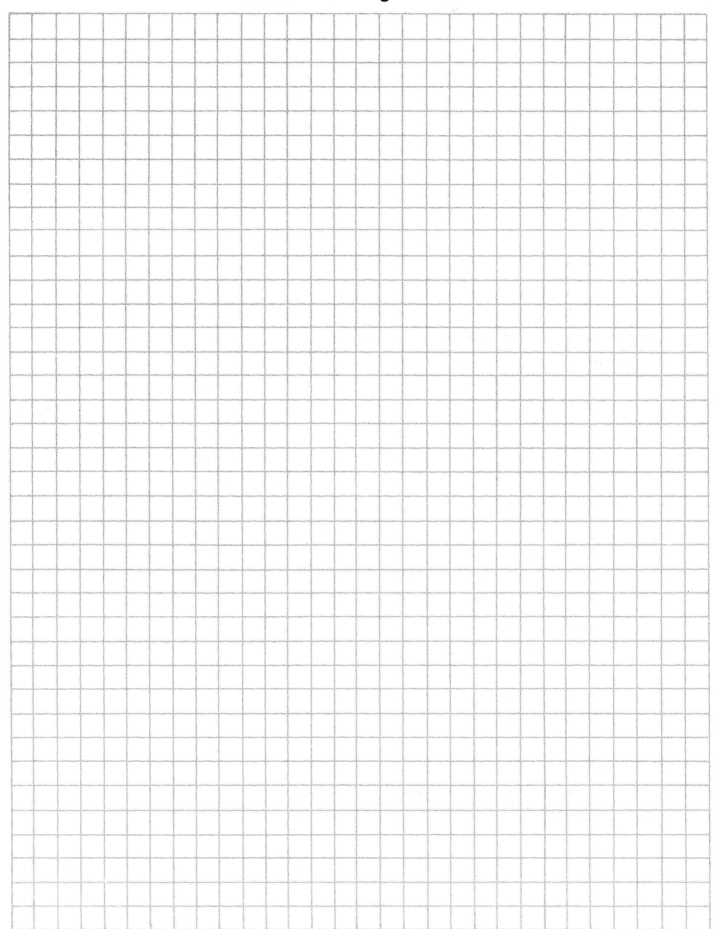

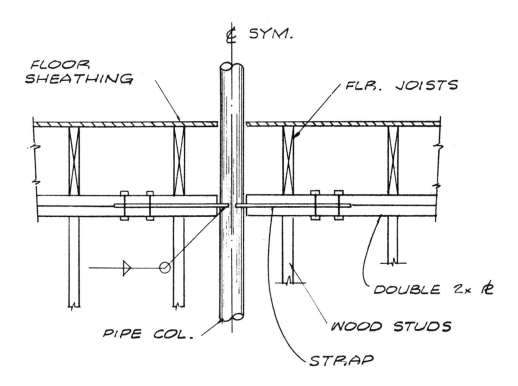

Detail 61. A steel pipe column connected to a wood stud wall. The connection is made to the double plates at the top of the wall to reduce the slenderness ratio of the pipe column. The connection is effective only in the direction parallel to the wall.

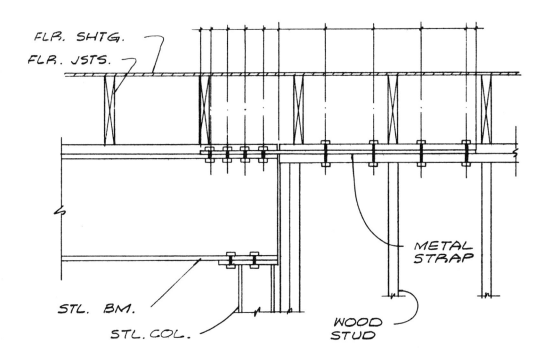

Detail 62. An end connection of a steel beam to a wood stud wall. The wood stud wall resists lateral forces that are transferred from the floor diaphragm to the steel beam. The lateral force is transferred to the wall through the metal strap that is bolted to the top flange of the beam and the double plates at the top of the wall. The strap may be welded to the beam in lieu of the bolts as shown.

Notes ▪ Drawings ▪ Ideas

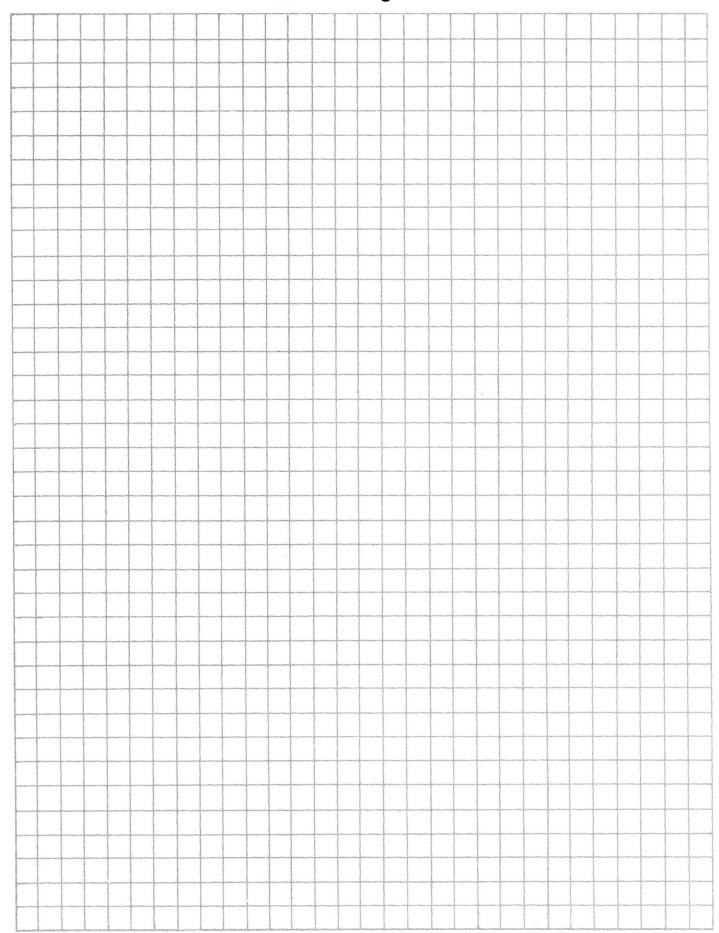

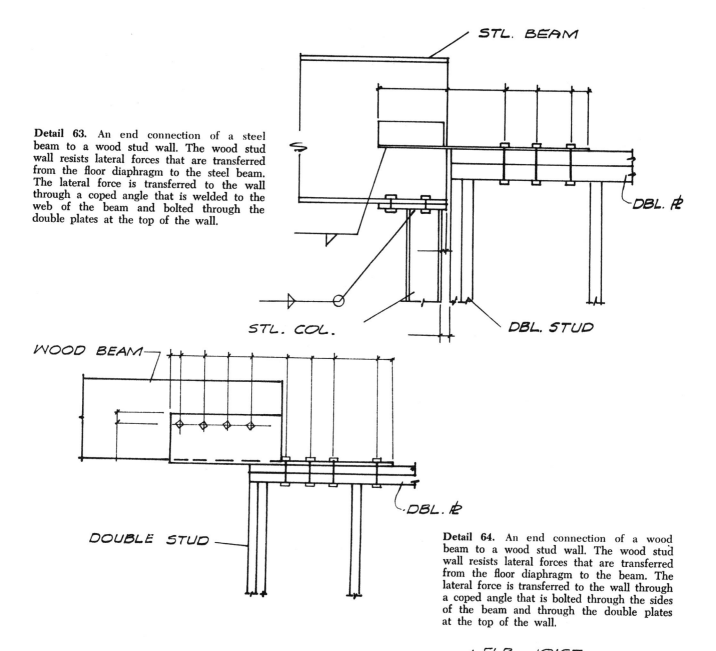

STL. BEAM

Detail 63. An end connection of a steel beam to a wood stud wall. The wood stud wall resists lateral forces that are transferred from the floor diaphragm to the steel beam. The lateral force is transferred to the wall through a coped angle that is welded to the web of the beam and bolted through the double plates at the top of the wall.

DBL. ℞

STL. COL.

DBL. STUD

WOOD BEAM

DBL. ℞

DOUBLE STUD

Detail 64. An end connection of a wood beam to a wood stud wall. The wood stud wall resists lateral forces that are transferred from the floor diaphragm to the beam. The lateral force is transferred to the wall through a coped angle that is bolted through the sides of the beam and through the double plates at the top of the wall.

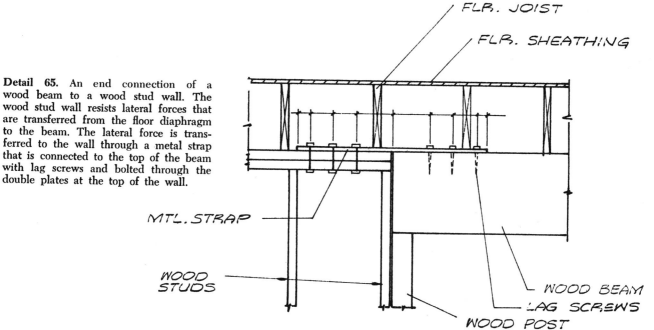

FLR. JOIST

FLR. SHEATHING

Detail 65. An end connection of a wood beam to a wood stud wall. The wood stud wall resists lateral forces that are transferred from the floor diaphragm to the beam. The lateral force is transferred to the wall through a metal strap that is connected to the top of the beam with lag screws and bolted through the double plates at the top of the wall.

MTL. STRAP

WOOD STUDS

WOOD BEAM

LAG SCREWS

WOOD POST

Notes ▪ Drawings ▪ Ideas

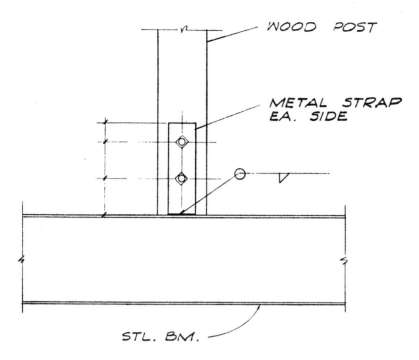

Detail 66(a). A wood post supported by a steel beam. The metal plates bolted through each side of the post are welded to the top flange of the beam.

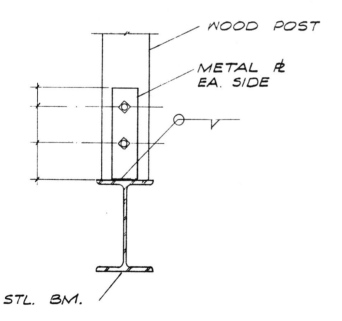

Detail 66(b). A wood post supported by a steel beam. The metal plates bolted through each side of the post are welded to the top flange of the beam.

Notes ▪ Drawings ▪ Ideas

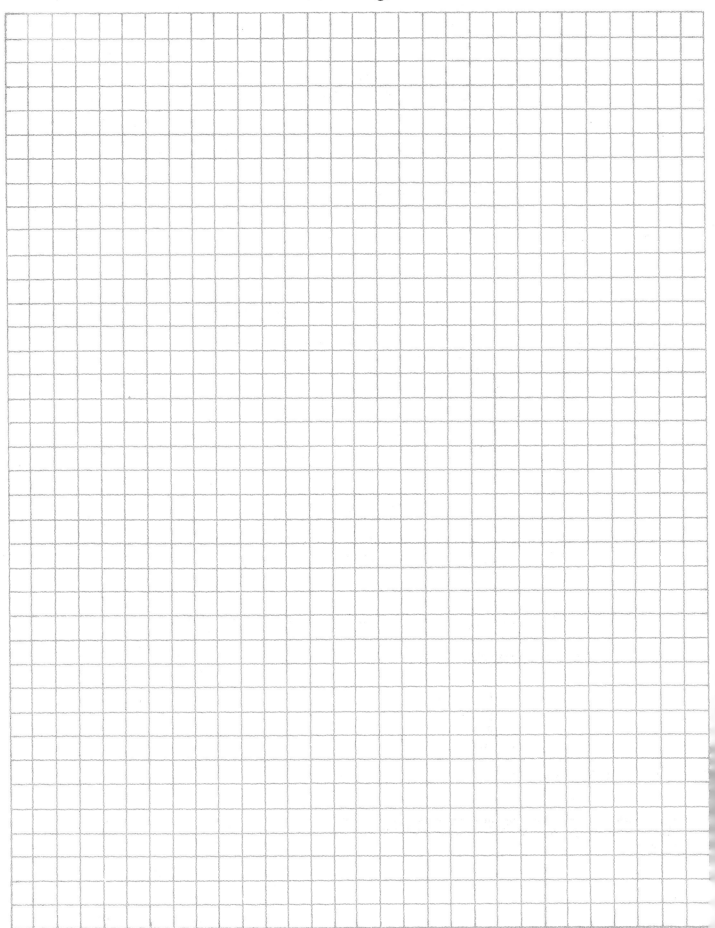

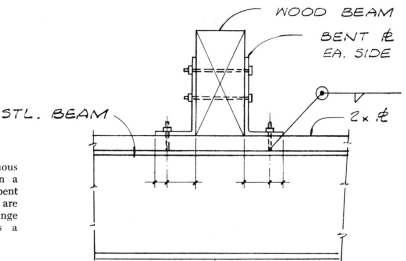

STL. BEAM

Detail 67(a). A connection of a continuous or cantilevered wood beam supported on a steel beam. The horizontal legs of the bent plates on each side of the wood beam are connected with bolts welded to the top flange of the steel beam. Detail 67(b) shows a section of this connection.

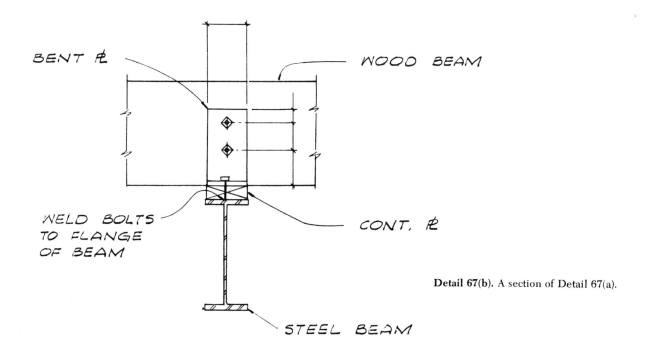

BENT ℞

WOOD BEAM

WELD BOLTS
TO FLANGE
OF BEAM

CONT. ℞

Detail 67(b). A section of Detail 67(a).

STEEL BEAM

Detail 68. An intersection connection of a wood beam to a steel beam. A metal plate is welded to the edges of the steel beam flanges as shown. A U-shaped metal plate is welded to the flat plate and bolted through the wood beam. The steel beam may require web stiffener plates depending on the wood beam reaction.

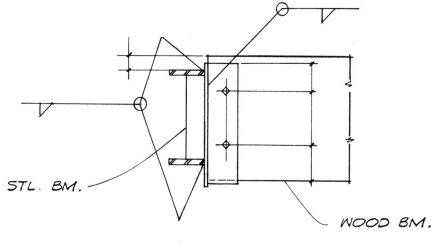

STL. BM.

WOOD BM.

81

Notes ▪ Drawings ▪ Ideas

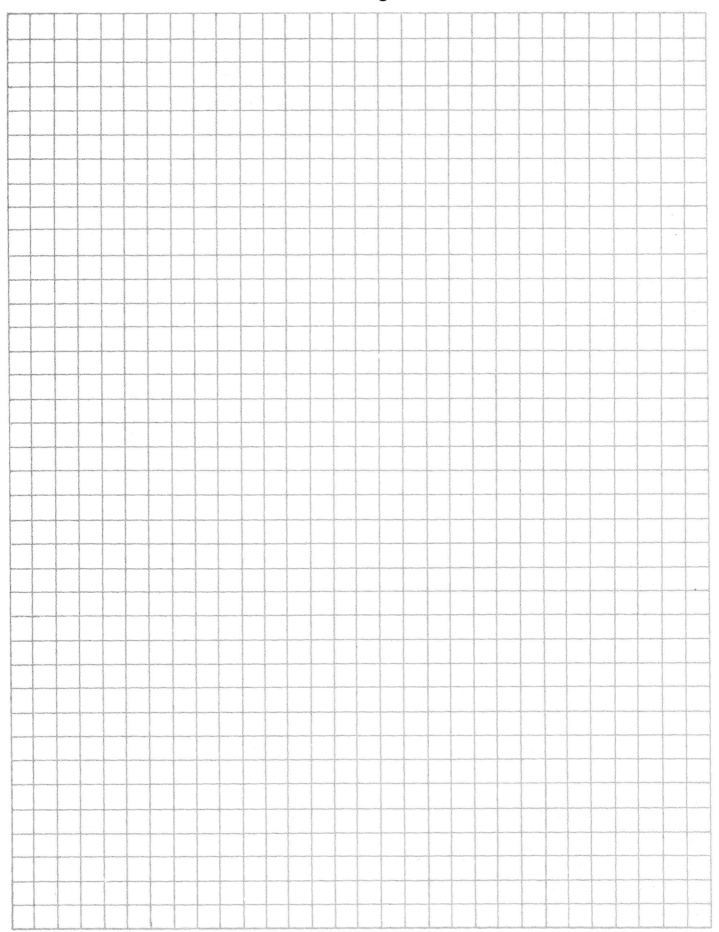

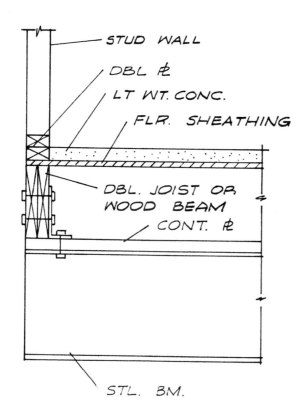

STUD WALL

DBL. Pℓ

LT WT. CONC.

FLR. SHEATHING

DBL. JOIST OR
WOOD BEAM

CONT. Pℓ

STL. BM.

Detail 69. A section of double wood floor joists supporting a wood stud wall on a steel beam. The double joist is connected to the steel beam by a clip angle that is bolted to the top flange of the beam with one bolt on each side of the beam web.

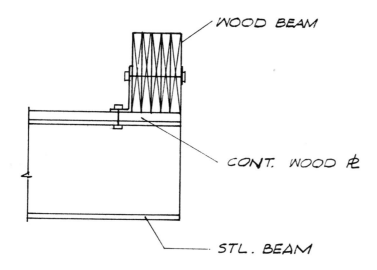

WOOD BEAM

CONT. WOOD Pℓ

STL. BEAM

Detail 70. A connection of a wood beam to the top of a steel beam. The laterally laminated wood beam is composed of 2″ wide members. See Detail 35(b). The wood beam is connected to the steel beam by a clip angle that is bolted to the top flange of the steel beam with one bolt on each side of the beam web.

Notes · Drawings · Ideas

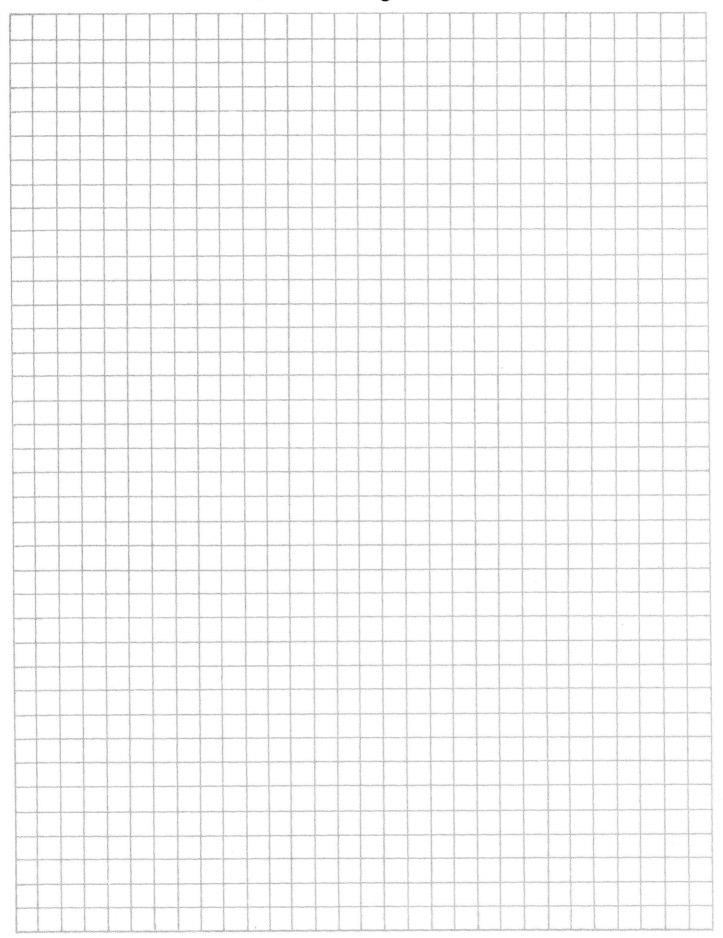

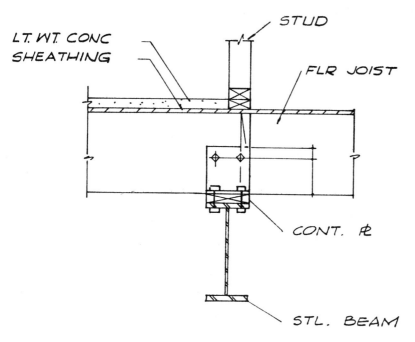

STUD

LT. WT. CONC SHEATHING

FLR JOIST

CONT. ℞

STL. BEAM

Detail 71. A section of a steel beam supporting cantilevered wood floor joists. The clip angles are spaced at 4'0" o.c. and connect the floor joists to the top of the steel beam. The clip angles have two bolts through each leg.

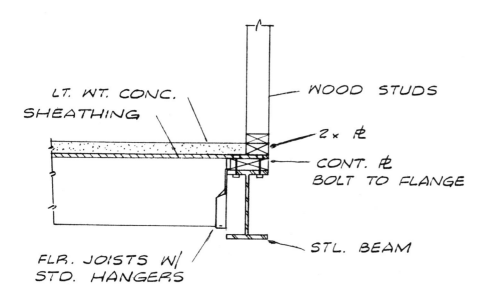

LT. WT. CONC. SHEATHING

WOOD STUDS

2 × ℞

CONT. ℞ BOLT TO FLANGE

STL. BEAM

FLR. JOISTS W/ STD. HANGERS

Detail 72. A section of a steel beam supporting an exterior wood stud wall, floor joists, and light-weight concrete on a wood floor. The floor joists are supported by the beam with standard joist hangers welded to the top flange. The wood nailer plate is bolted to the top flange of the beam with ⅝" dia. bolts spaced at 4'0" o.c., staggered on each side of the beam web. The double plate of the stud wall on the floor is optional; a single plate may be used.

Notes ▪ Drawings ▪ Ideas

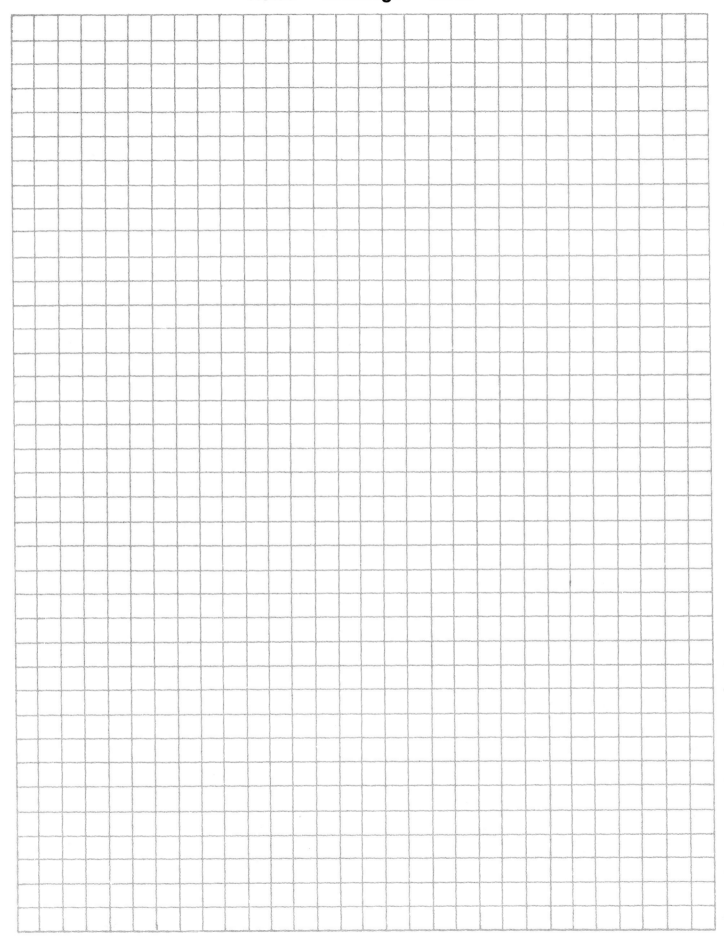

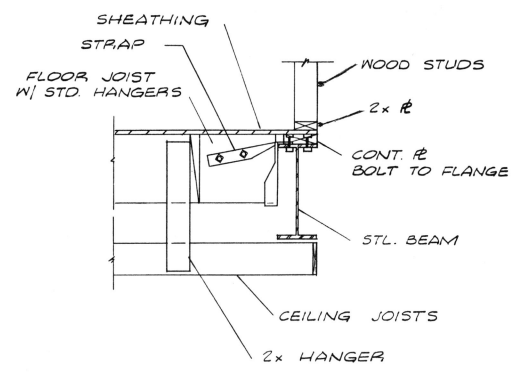

SHEATHING

STRAP

FLOOR JOIST
W/ STD. HANGERS

WOOD STUDS

2 x ℔

CONT. ℔
BOLT TO FLANGE

STL. BEAM

CEILING JOISTS

2 x HANGER

Detail 73. A section of a steel beam supporting an exterior wood stud wall, floor joists, and a suspended ceiling. The detail is similar to Detail 72. The ceiling joists are suspended from the floor joists by a wood hanger. The hanger spacing determines the span of the ceiling joists.

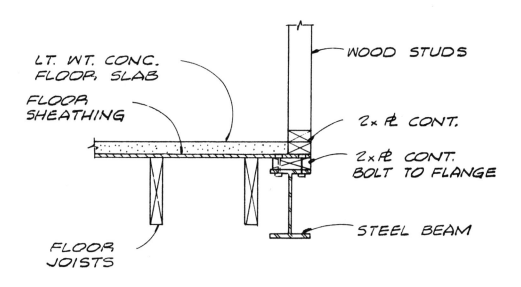

LT. WT. CONC.
FLOOR SLAB

FLOOR
SHEATHING

WOOD STUDS

2 x ℔ CONT.

2 x ℔ CONT.
BOLT TO FLANGE

STEEL BEAM

FLOOR
JOISTS

Detail 74. A section of a steel beam supporting an exterior wood stud wall, floor joists, and light-weight concrete on a wood floor. The floor joists span parallel to the steel beam. The wood nailer plate is bolted to the top flange of the beam with ⅝" dia. bolts spaced at 4'0" o.c., staggered on each side of the beam web. The double plate of the stud wall on the floor is optional; a single plate may be used.

Notes ▪ Drawings ▪ Ideas

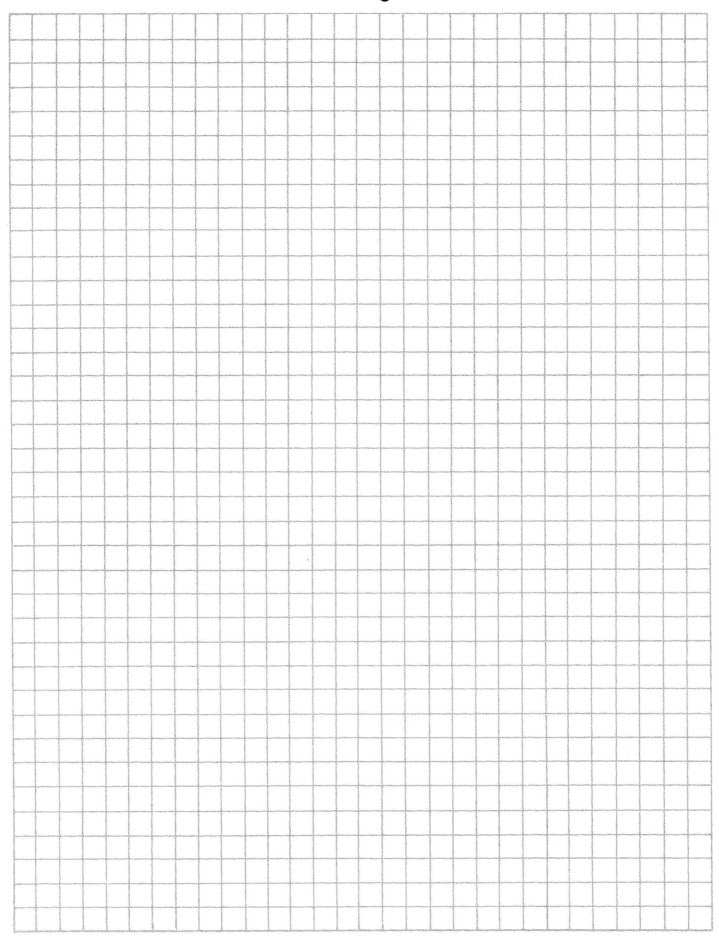

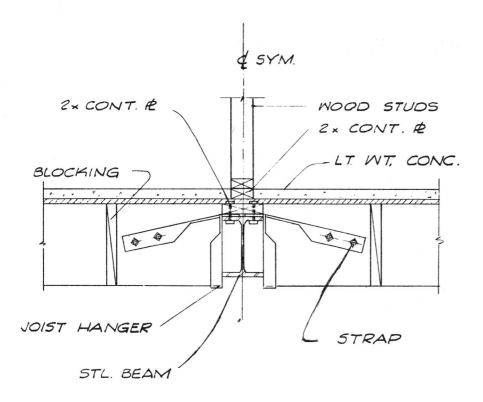

Detail 75. A section of a steel beam supporting an interior wood stud wall, floor joists, and light-weight concrete on a wood floor. The joists are supported by the beam with standard joist hangers welded to the top flange. The wood nailer plate is bolted to the top flange of the beam with ⅝″ dia. bolts spaced at 4′0″ o.c., staggered on each side of the beam web. A twisted metal strap or coped angle spaced at 4′0″ o.c. is welded to each side of the beam and bolted to a joist to transfer the floor diaphragm stress to the steel beam.

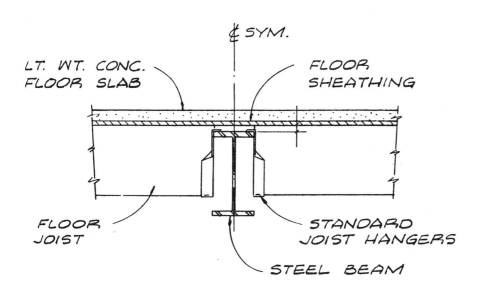

Detail 76. A section of a steel beam supporting wood floor joists and light-weight concrete on the wood floor. The floor joists are supported by the beam with standard joist hangers welded to the top flange. A space is provided between the top flange of the steel beam and the bottom side of the floor sheathing to allow for the wood shrinkage.

Notes · Drawings · Ideas

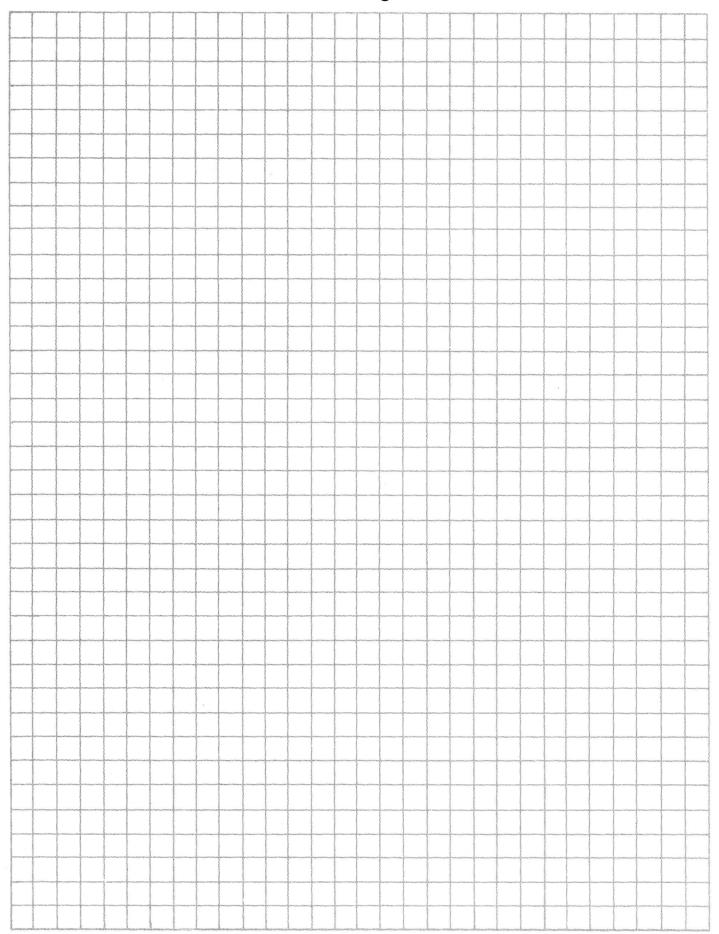

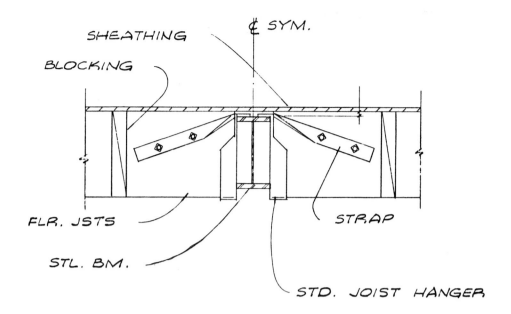

SHEATHING

BLOCKING

℄ SYM.

FLR. JSTS

STRAP

STL. BM.

STD. JOIST HANGER

Detail 77. A section of a steel beam supporting wood floor joists and a wood floor. The floor joists are supported by the beam with standard joist hangers welded to the top flange. A twisted metal strap spaced at 4'0" o.c. is welded to each side of the beam and bolted to a joist to transfer the floor diaphragm stress to the beam. A space is provided between the top flange of the steel beam and the bottom side of the floor sheathing to allow for the wood shrinkage.

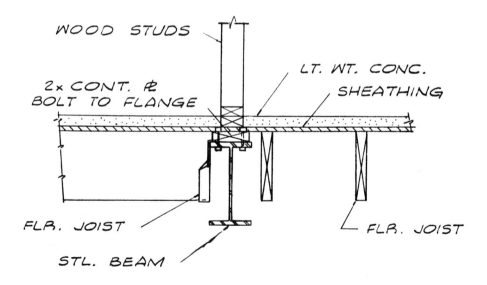

WOOD STUDS

LT. WT. CONC.

SHEATHING

2× CONT. ℔ BOLT TO FLANGE

FLR. JOIST

FLR. JOIST

STL. BEAM

Detail 78. A section of a steel beam supporting an interior wood stud wall, floor joists, and light-weight concrete on a wood floor. The floor joists on the left side of the beam are supported by the beam with standard joist hangers welded to the top flange. The floor joists on the right side of the beam span parallel to the beam. The wood nailer plate is bolted to the top flange of the beam with ⅝" dia. bolts spaced at 4'0" o.c., staggered on each side of the beam web. The double wood plate of the stud wall on the floor is optional; a single plate may be used.

Notes ▪ Drawings ▪ Ideas

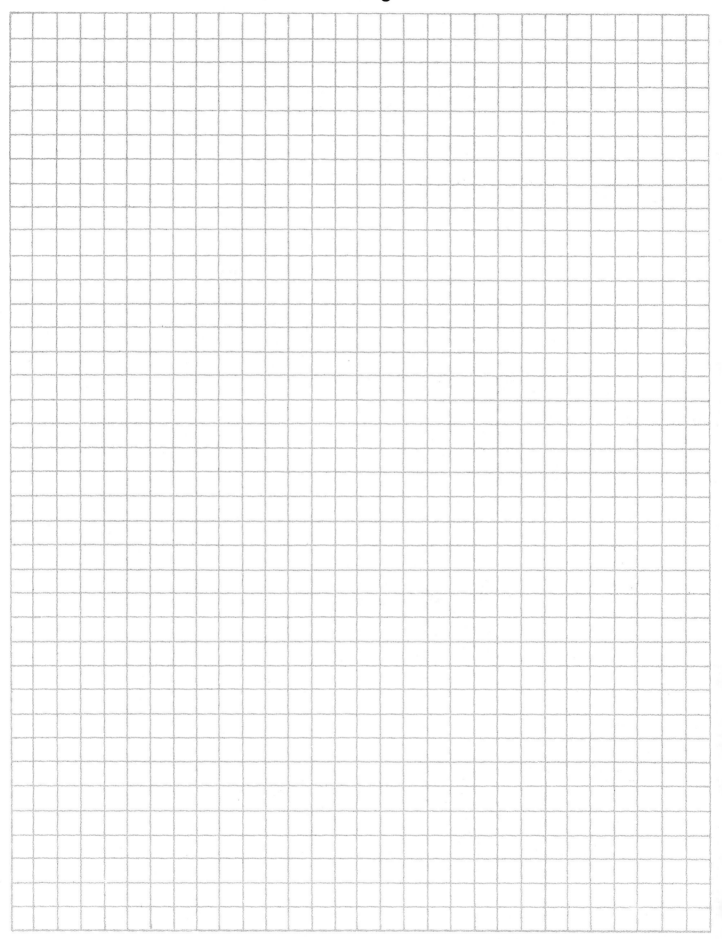

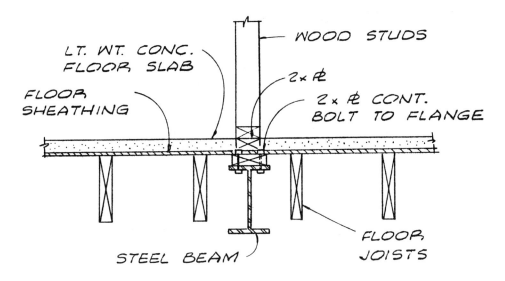

Detail 79. A section of a steel beam supporting an interior wood stud wall and light-weight concrete on a wood floor. The floor joists span parallel to the beam. The wood nailer plate is bolted to the top flange of the beam with ⅝″ dia. bolts spaced at 4′0″ o.c., staggered on each side of the beam web. The double plate of the stud wall on the floor is optional; a single plate may be used.

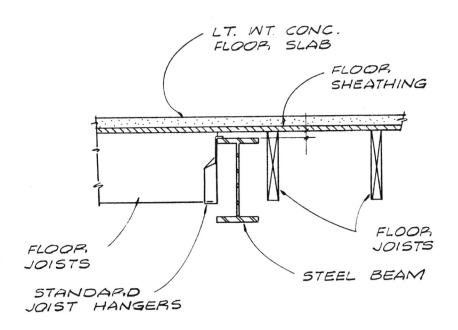

Detail 80. A section of a steel beam supporting floor joists and light-weight concrete on a wood floor. The floor joists on the left side are supported by the beam with standard joist hangers welded to the top flange. The floor joists on the right side span parallel to the beam. A space is provided between the top flange of the steel beam and the bottom side of the floor sheathing to allow for the wood shrinkage.

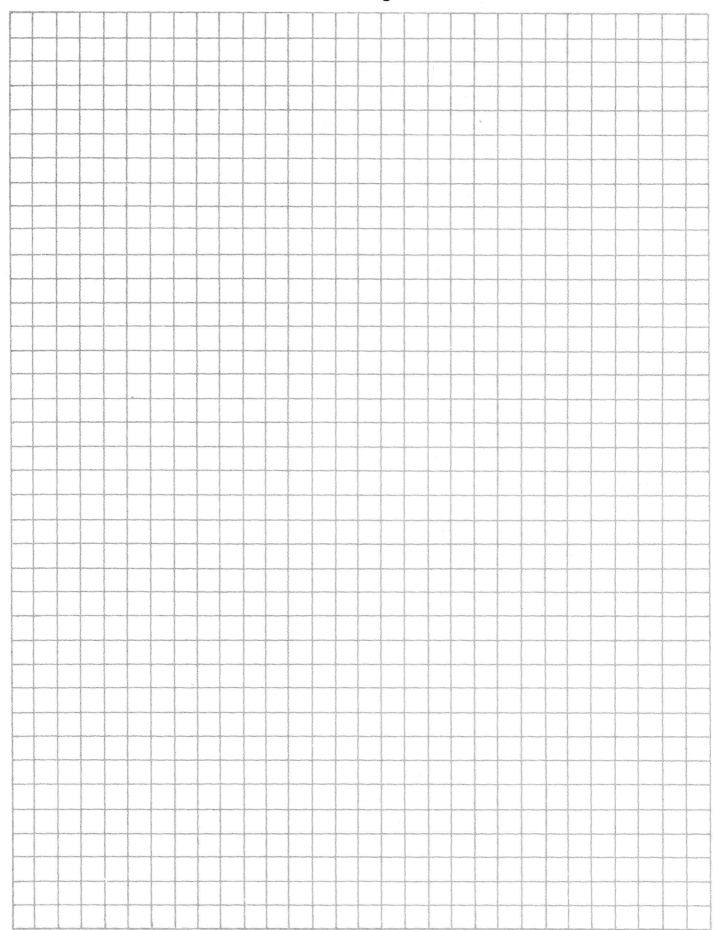

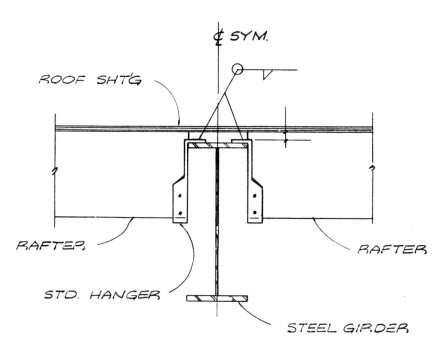

Detail 81(a). A section of a roof girder supporting wood rafters and roof sheathing. The rafters are supported by the girder with standard joist hangers welded to the top flange. A space is provided between the top flange of the steel girder and the bottom side of the sheathing to allow for the wood shrinkage.

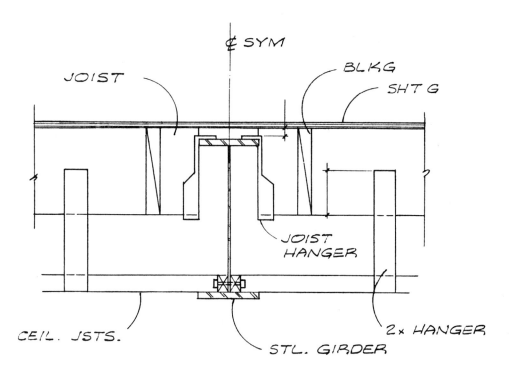

Detail 81(b). A section of a roof girder as shown in Detail 81(a) and a suspended ceiling. The ceiling joists are suspended from the rafters by wood hangers. The hanger spacing determines the span of the ceiling joists.

Notes ▪ Drawings ▪ Ideas

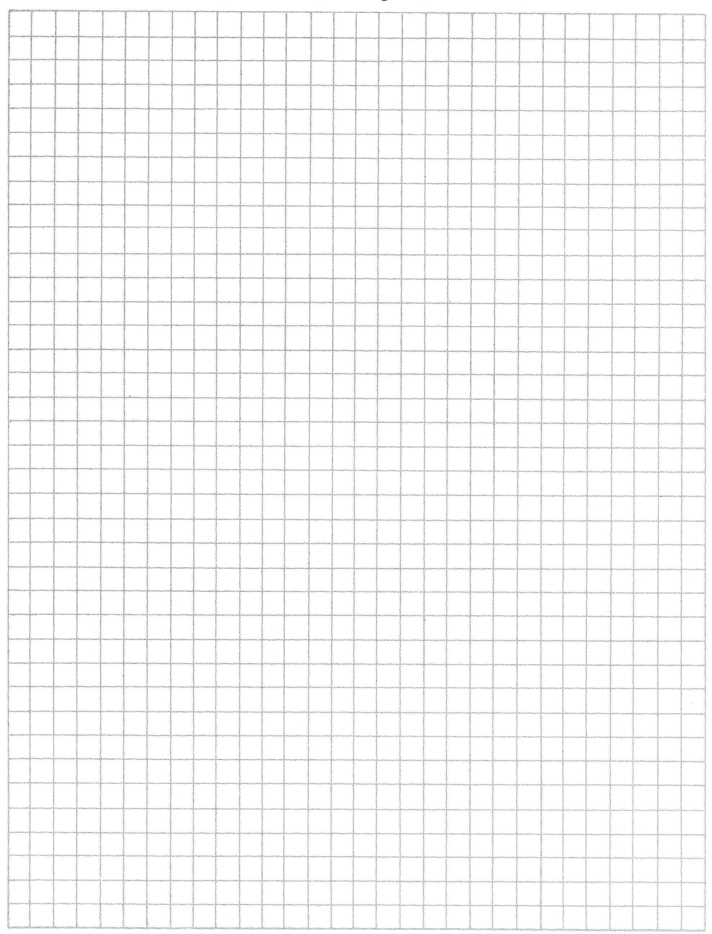

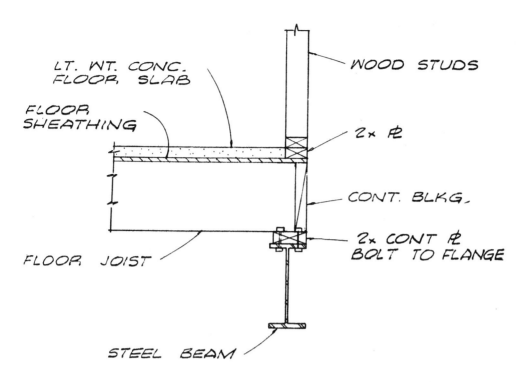

Detail 82(a). A section of a steel beam supporting an exterior wood stud wall, wood floor joists, and light-weight concrete on a wood floor. The joists are continuously blocked and bear on the nailer plate. The wood nailer plate is bolted to the top flange of the beam with ⅝" dia. bolts spaced at 4'0" o.c., staggered on each side of the beam web. The double plate of the stud wall on the floor is optional; a single plate may be used.

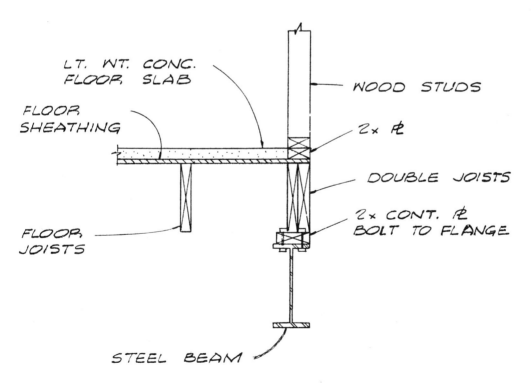

Detail 82(b). A section of a steel beam supporting an exterior wood stud wall and light-weight concrete on a wood floor. The joists span parallel to the beam. The double joists support the wood stud wall on the beam. The wood nailer plate is bolted to the top flange of the beam with ⅝" dia. bolts spaced at 4'0" o.c., staggered on each side of the beam web. The double plate of the stud wall on the floor is optional; a single plate may be used.

Notes ▪ Drawings ▪ Ideas

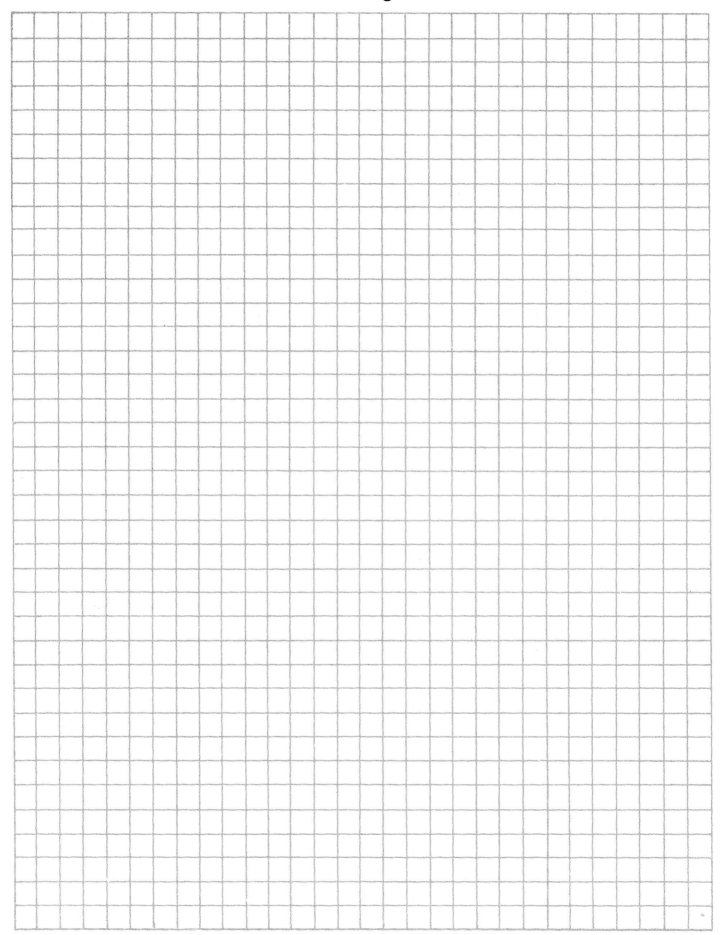

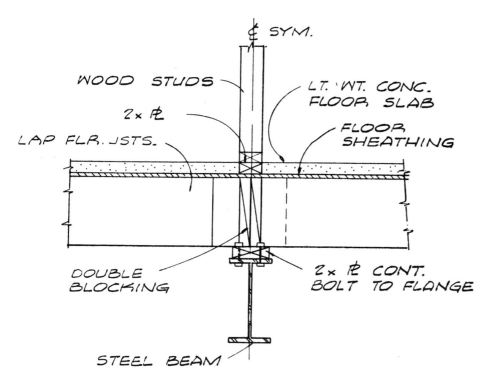

Detail 83. A section of a steel beam supporting an interior wood stud wall, floor joists, and light-weight concrete on a wood floor. The floor joists are lapped and bear on the top flange wood nailer. The continuous double blocking transfers the floor diaphragm stress to the beam. The wood nailer plate is bolted to the top flange of the beam with ⅝" dia. bolts spaced at 4'0" o.c., staggered on each side of the beam web. The double plate of the stud wall on the floor is optional; a single plate may be used.

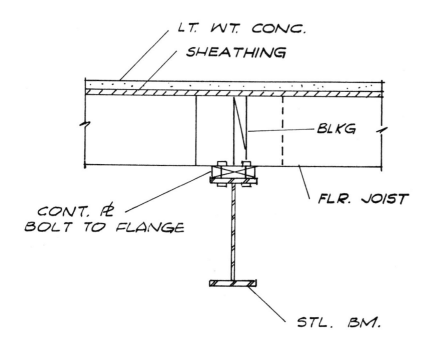

Detail 84. A section of a steel beam supporting wood floor joists and light-weight concrete on a wood floor. The joists are lapped and blocked and bear on the wood nailer at the top flange of the beam. The wood nailer plate is bolted to the top flange of the beam with ⅝" dia. bolts spaced at 4'0" o.c., staggered on each side of the beam web.

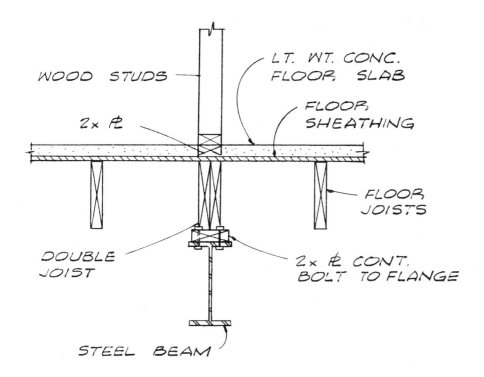

WOOD STUDS

2× ℞

DOUBLE JOIST

STEEL BEAM

LT. WT. CONC. FLOOR SLAB

FLOOR SHEATHING

FLOOR JOISTS

2× ℞ CONT. BOLT TO FLANGE

Detail 85(a). A section of a steel beam supporting an interior wood stud wall, wood floor joists, and light-weight concrete on a wood floor. The floor joists on the right side span parallel to the beam. The double continuous blocking transfers the floor diaphragm stress to the steel beam. The wood nailer plate is bolted to the top flange of the beam with ⅝″ dia. bolts spaced at 4′0″ o.c., staggered on each side of the beam web. The double plate of the stud wall on the floor is optional; a single plate may be used.

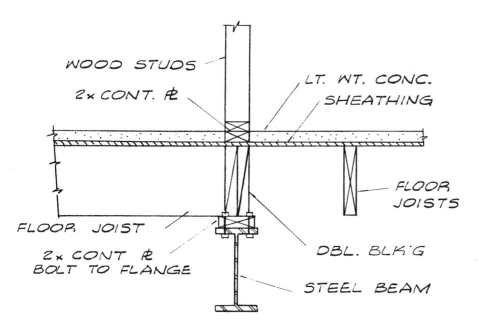

WOOD STUDS

2× CONT. ℞

FLOOR JOIST

2× CONT ℞ BOLT TO FLANGE

LT. WT. CONC. SHEATHING

FLOOR JOISTS

DBL. BLK'G

STEEL BEAM

Detail 85(b). A section of a steel beam supporting an interior wood stud wall and light-weight concrete on a wood floor. The floor joists span parallel to the beam. The double joists transfer the weight of the wood stud wall to the beam. The wood nailer plate is bolted to the top flange of the beam with ⅝″ dia. bolts spaced at 4′0″ o.c., staggered on each side of the beam web. The double plate of the stud wall on the floor is optional; a single plate may be used.

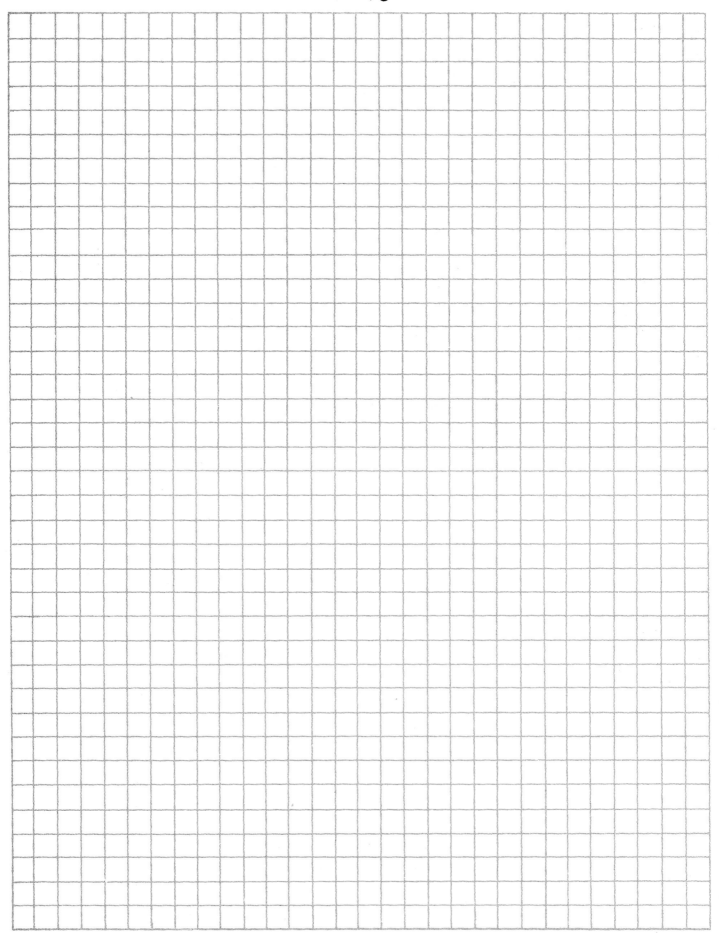

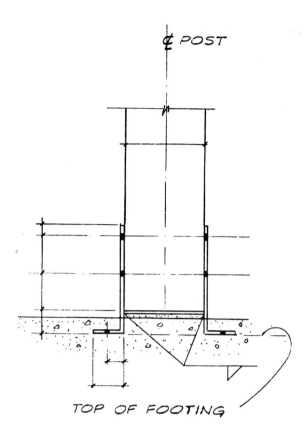

Detail 86(a). A connection of a glued laminated wood post to a concrete foundation. See Detail 86(b).

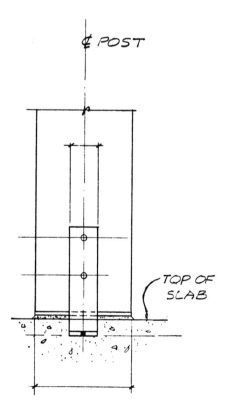

Detail 86(b). A side view of the metal connection plates shown in Detail 86(a).

Notes ▪ Drawings ▪ Ideas

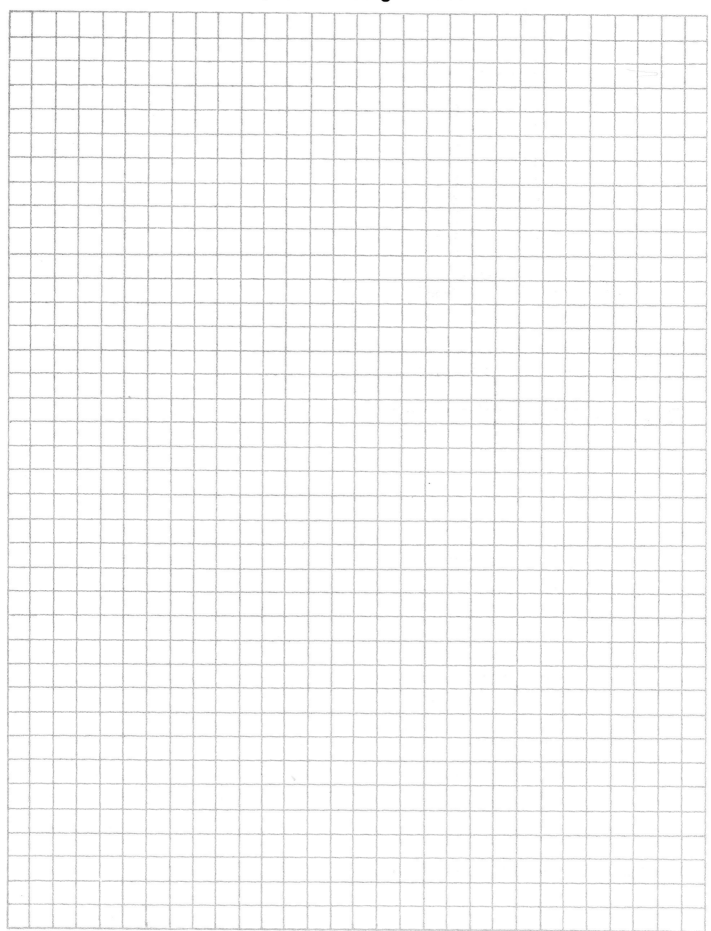

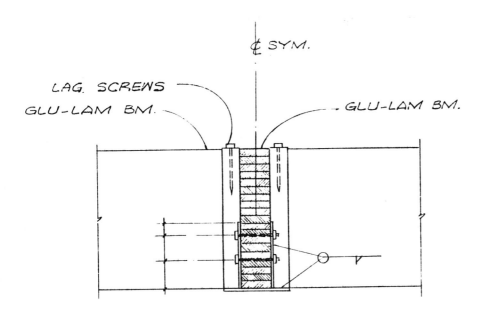

Detail 87(a). An intersection of two glued laminated wood beams. The beam shown in section is supported by the beam shown in elevation. A metal strap hanger is connected to the top of the supporting beam with lag screws and bolted through the sides of the beam shown in section. See Detail 87(b).

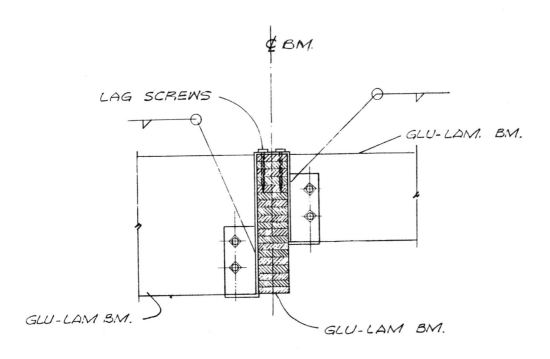

Detail 87(b). A section of Detail 87(a). The beams on each side of the supporting beam are shown in elevation. The metal strap hanger plates are designed to act in tension.

Notes ▪ Drawings ▪ Ideas

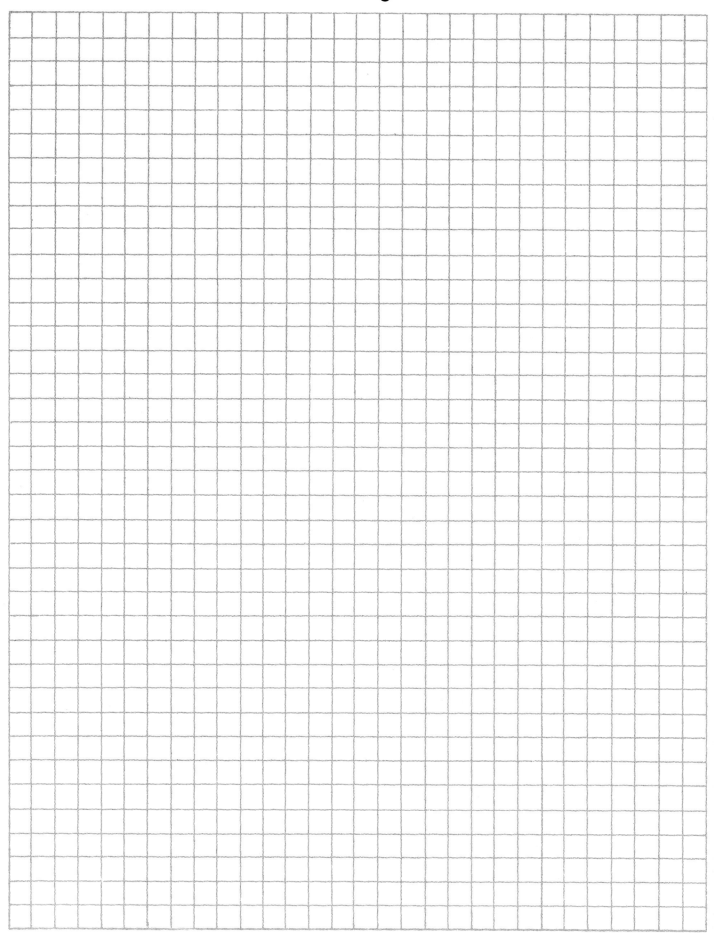

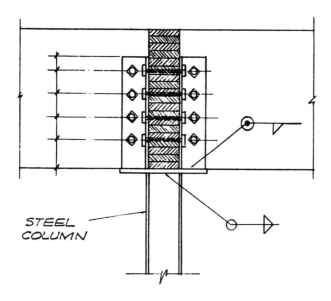

Detail 88(a). A wide flange steel column supporting the intersection of four glued laminated wood beams. See Detail 88(b).

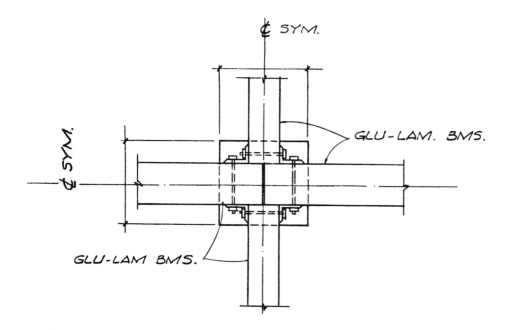

Detail 88(b). A plan of Detail 88(a) showing the intersection of four glued laminated wood beams on a wide flange steel column. The beams are connected with clip angles and bolts. The angles are welded to the cap plate at the top of the column.

Notes ▪ Drawings ▪ Ideas

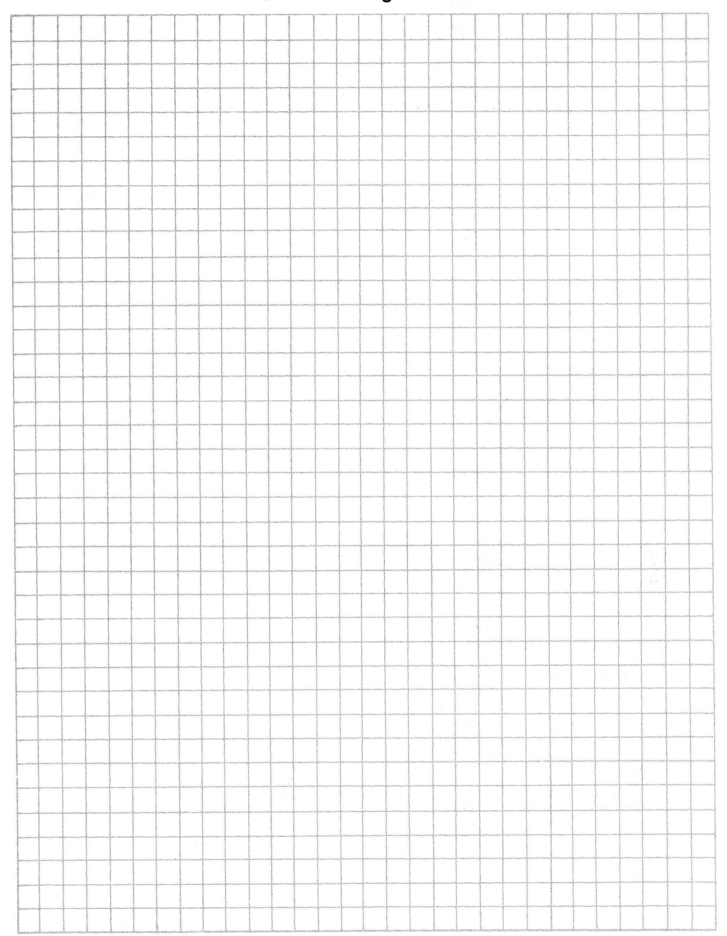

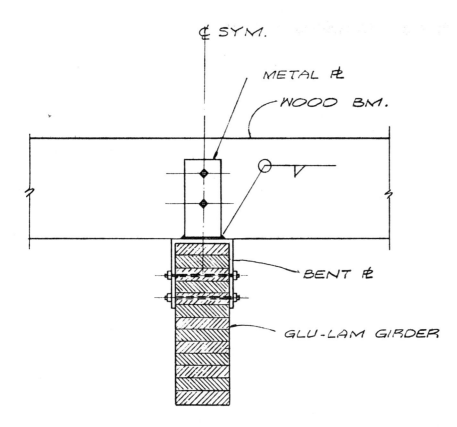

Detail 89(a). A section of a glued laminated wood girder supporting a glued laminated wood beam. The beam is connected to the top of the girder by metal side plates bolted through the girder and through the beam. See Detail 89(b).

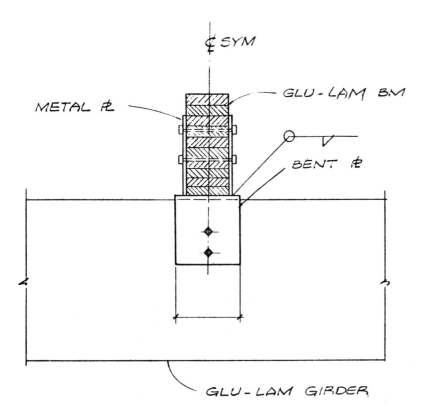

Detail 89(b). A section of Detail 89(a) showing the glued laminated wood beam in section.

Notes ▪ Drawings ▪ Ideas

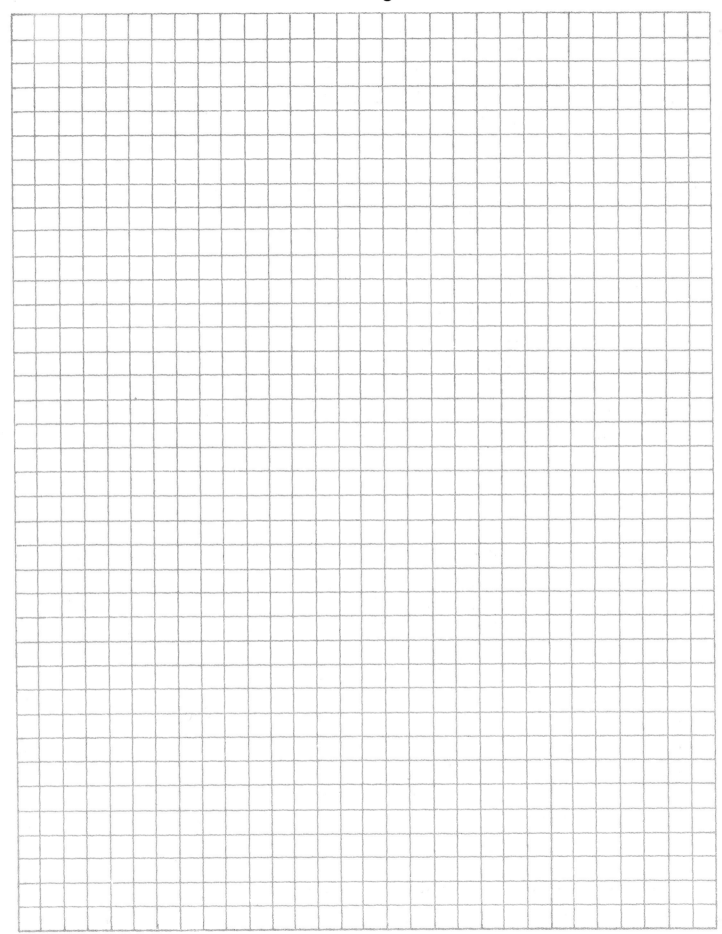

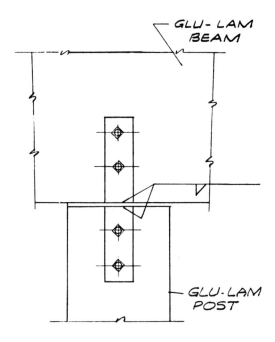

Detail 90(a). A connection of a continuous glued laminated wood beam and a wood post. The metal side plates are bolted through the beam and through the post. The side plates are welded to the horizontal plate at the top of the post. See Detail 90(b).

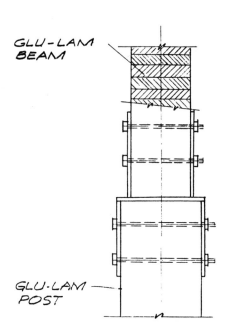

Detail 90(b). A section of Detail 90(a).

Notes · Drawings · Ideas

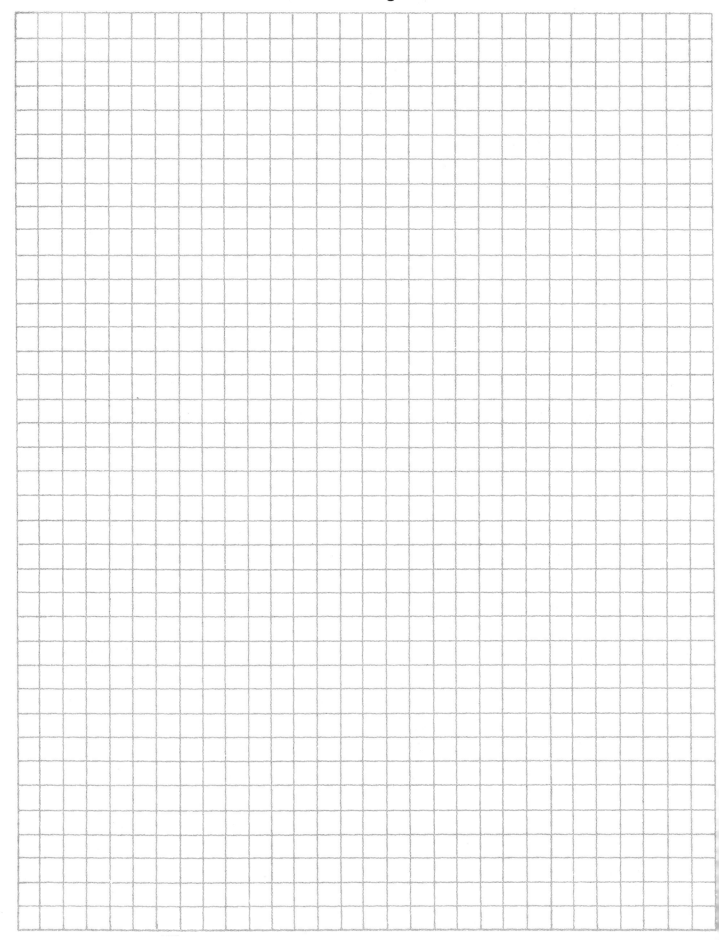

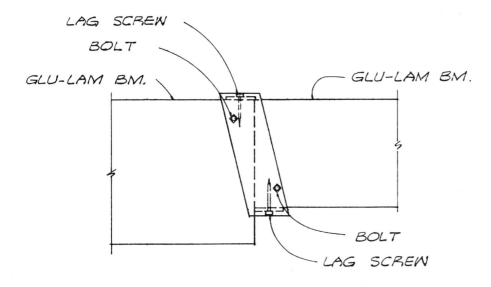

Detail 91(a). A connection of two glued laminated wood beams. The metal strap hanger is connected to the top of the left beam and suspends the end of the right beam. The beams are equal in width. See Detail 91(b).

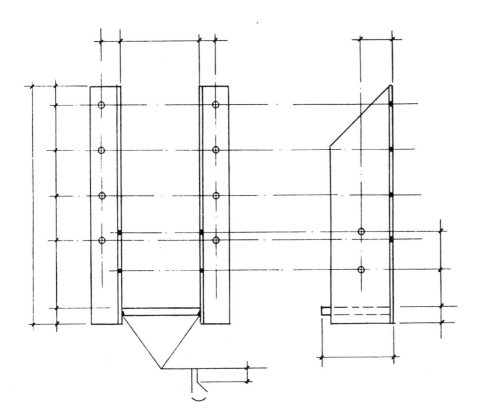

Detail 91(b). Two views of a metal strap hanger used in Detail 91(a). The hanger is bolted through the sides of the beams and lag screwed at top and bottom of the beams.

Notes · Drawings · Ideas

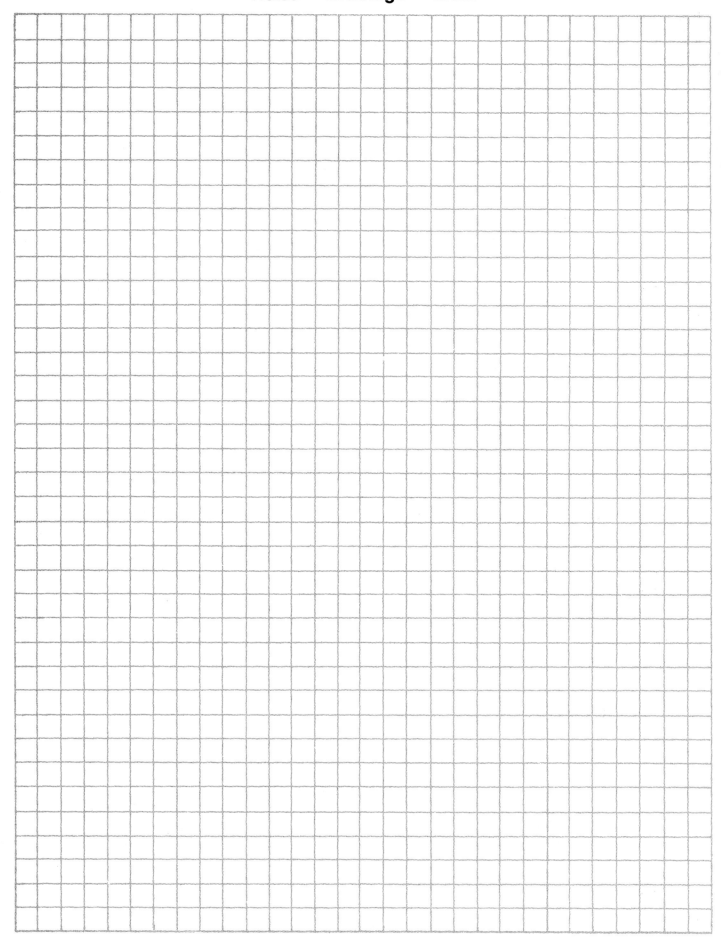

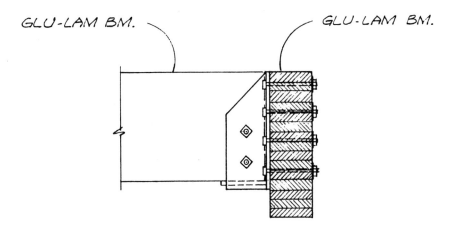

GLU-LAM BM.　　　　　　　　GLU-LAM BM.

Detail 92(a). A connection of a glued laminated wood beam supported by a glued laminated wood girder. The beam is connected to the girder with metal angle plates and a shelf plate. See Detail 92(b).

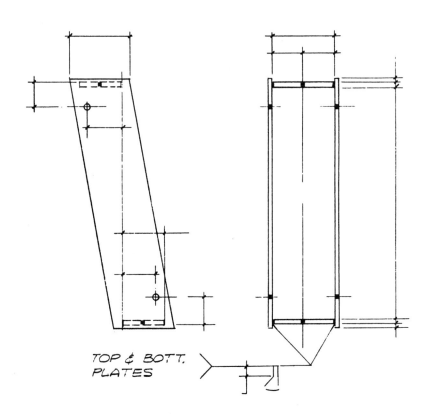

TOP & BOTT.
PLATES

Detail 92(b). Two views of the connecting angles and shelf plate used in Detail 92(a). The size of the plates and bolts used to connect the beam to the girder is determined by calculation.

Notes ▪ Drawings ▪ Ideas

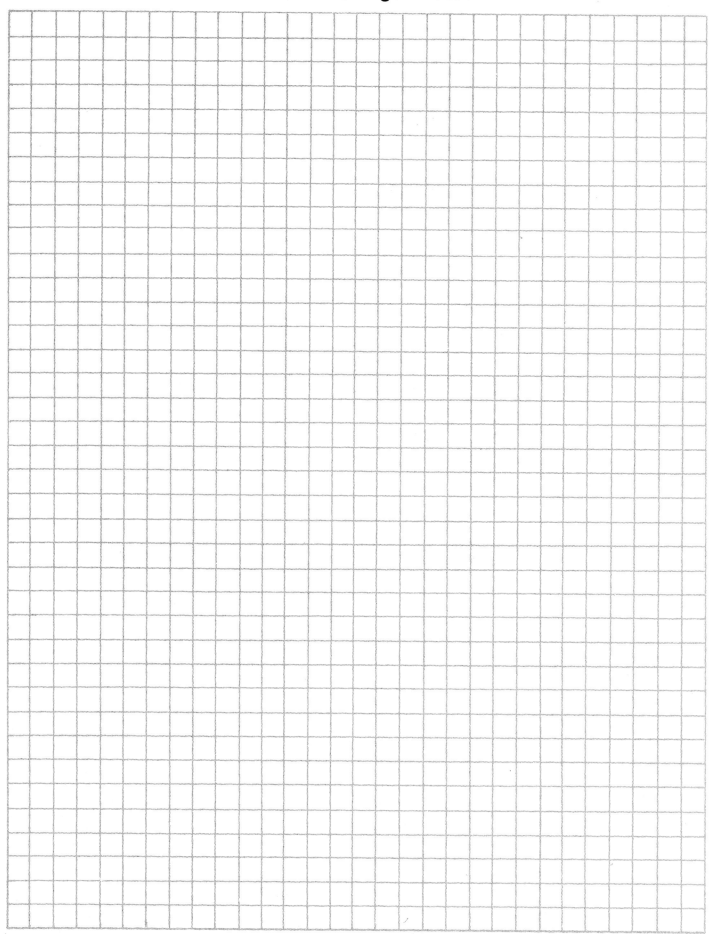

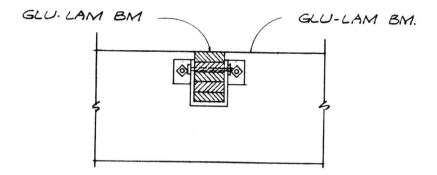

Detail 93(a). A connection of a wood purlin to a glued laminated wood beam. See Detail 93(b).

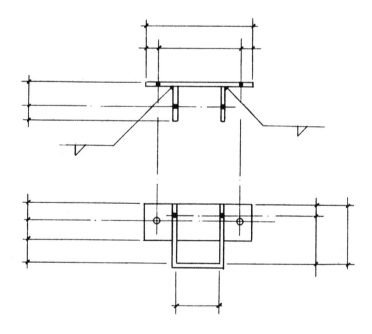

Detail 93(b). Two views of the connecting plates shown in Detail 93(a). The sizes of the plates and bolts used to connect the purlin to the beam are determined by calculation.

Notes · Drawings · Ideas

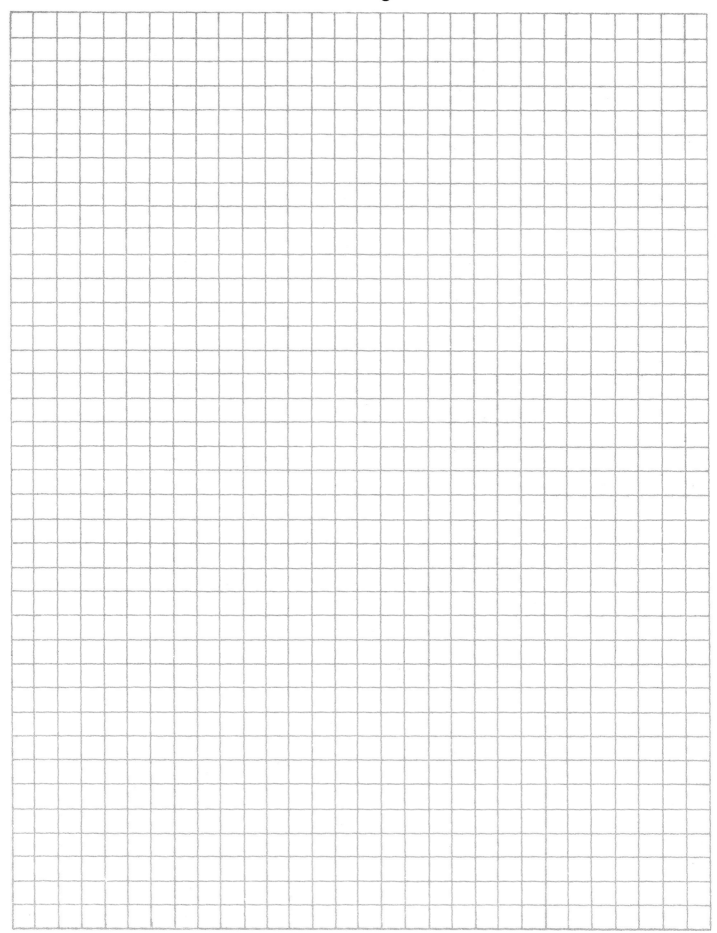

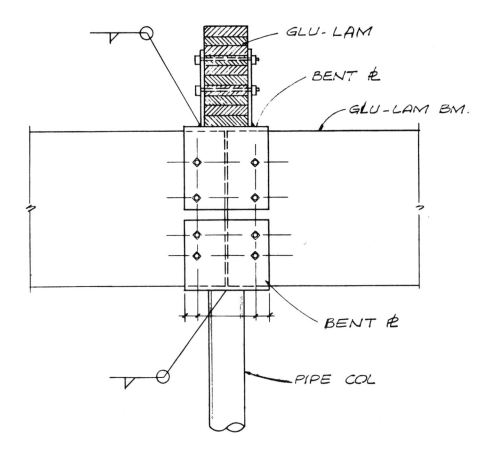

GLU-LAM

BENT ℞

GLU-LAM BM.

BENT ℞

PIPE COL

Detail 94. A connection of a glued laminated wood beam and girder supported by a steel pipe column. The beams are connected to the girder similar to Detail 89(a). The pipe column is connected to the wood girder similar to Detail 49(a).

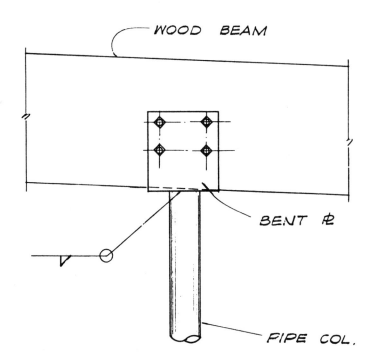

WOOD BEAM

BENT ℞

PIPE COL.

Detail 95. A steel pipe column supporting a cantilevered glued laminated wood beam. The beam is connected to the pipe column similar to Detail 49(a).

INDEX

Anchor(s), seismic, 9
  for wood posts, 9–13, 103

Beams, concrete:
  connected to a stud wall, 77
  and pipe column cantilever connection, 63
  and pipe column connection, 61–71
  and pipe column end connection, 51, 55
  and steel wide flange column connection, 61, 73
  and steel wide flange column end connection, 51, 55, 57
  and structural steel tube column end connection, 57, 73
  wood, laterally laminated, 43
    for wall and floor sections, 37, 43
  and wood post connection, 59, 65–69
  and wood post end connection, 47–53
  and wood stair stringer connection, 23
Bridging for wood floors and roofs, 17

Cantilevered beams, glued laminated wood, 119
  pipe column connection to wood, 63
  wide flange connection to wood, 63
  wood post connection to wood, 65, 69

Diagonal wood sheathing plan, 15

Equipment platform, wood, 45
Exterior wood stud wall and framing, 23–27
Exterior wood stud wall supported by a steel beam, 83–87, 97
Exterior wood stud wall supported by a wood beam, 37, 39

Floors (see Wood floor)

Glued laminated wood:
  beam connections, 105
  beam and girder connection, 109, 115, 119
  beam and post connection, 111
  beam and purlin connection, 111
  beam and wide flange column connection, 107
  hanger support connection, 113

Glued laminated wood (Cont.):
  intersection connection of beams, 105, 109, 115
  intersection, connection at a column, 107, 111, 119

Hip roof, wood framing, 67
Horizontal diaphragm, diagonal sheathing, 15
  plywood, 17

Interior steel stud wall and wood floor framing, 33
Interior wood stud wall:
  supported by a wood beam, 37, 41, 43
  supported by a steel beam, 89–93, 99, 101
  and wood floor framing, 31

Joists, wood (see Wood floor)

Laterally laminated wood beams, 43
Ledger bolts, 45, 85

Masonry wall wood ledger bolts, 45

Non-bearing walls, wood studs, to floor joist connection, 29

Partitions connected to wood floors, 29
Plywood floor and roof diaphragm, 17
Purlin and wood ledger elevation, 45

Roof platform, 45
Roof wood sheathing (see Diagonal wood sheathing plan; Plywood floor and roof diaphragm)

Seismic connection of wood wall to beams, 75, 77
Seismic wood wall tie down, 15
Stairs, 21, 23
Steel beam:
  cantilevered connection to a wood post, 65, 69
  end connection to a wood post, 51, 53
  supporting wood beam, 81, 83
  supporting wood floor joists, 85
  and wood wall, 85–93

Steel beam (Cont.):
  supporting wood post, 79
Steel column, cantilevered wood beam connection, 63
  glued laminated wood beam connections, 107
  wood beam connections, 61, 73
Steel girder and wood rafter, section, 95
Steel pipe columns, cantilevered wood beam connection, 63
  glued laminated wood beam connection, 119
  wood beam connection, 51, 55, 61, 69, 71
  wood stud wall top plates, 75
Steel stud walls, and wood floor, 27–33
  and wood rafters, 35

Wide flange steel columns:
  and cantilevered wood beam, 63
  connected to wood beams, 51, 55, 57, 61, 73
  and glued laminated wood beam, 107
Wood:
  glued laminated (see Glued laminated wood)
  plywood (see Plywood floor and roof diaphragm; Horizontal diaphragm, plywood)
Wood beam:
  and pipe column connection, 61, 69, 71
  and pipe column end connection, 63
  and post connection, 59, 65–69
  and post end connection, 47, 49
  and steel tube end connection, 73
  supported by a steel beam, 81, 83
  and wide flange steel column cantilever connection, 63
  and wide flange steel column connection, 61, 73
  and wood wall section, 37–41
Wood floor:
  and bridging, 17
  and concrete surface, 19, 21
  and diagonal sheathing, 17
  and partition connection, 17
  and plywood sheathing, 17
  and steel beam section, 83–99

Wood floor (*Cont.*):
    and steel stud wall section, 27,
      33
    and wood beam sections, 37−43
    and wood walls, 25−31
Wood ledger, 45
Wood partitions (*see* Partitions connected
    to wood floors)
Wood post connections:
    to base plates, 9−13, 103

Wood post connections (*Cont.*):
    to cantilevered steel beam 65, 69
    to concrete footings, 9−13
    to steel beam, 47−53, 59, 65, 67
Wood purlin and glued laminated beam,
    117
Wood roof:
    and steel girder section, 95
    and wood parapet wall, 23, 25
Wood roof platform, 45

Wood stairs, 21, 23
Wood stud walls:
    and beam and floor sections, 37-43
    and parapet, 23, 25
    and pipe column connection, 75
    and seismic connection to beams, 75,
      77
    and seismic tie down, 15
    and steel beam sections, 83−101
    and top plate splice, 37